Career Paths

Charting Courses to Success for Organizations and Their Employees

Gary W. Carter, Kevin W. Cook, and
David W. Dorsey

WILEY-BLACKWELL

A John Wiley & Sons, Ltd., Publication

This edition first published 2009
© 2009 Gary W. Carter, Kevin W. Cook, and David W. Dorsey

Blackwell Publishing was acquired by John Wiley & Sons in February 2007. Blackwell's publishing program has been merged with Wiley's global Scientific, Technical, and Medical business to form Wiley-Blackwell.

Registered Office
John Wiley & Sons Ltd, The Atrium, Southern Gate, Chichester, West Sussex, PO19 8SQ, United Kingdom

Editorial Offices
350 Main Street, Malden, MA 02148-5020, USA
9600 Garsington Road, Oxford, OX4 2DQ, UK
The Atrium, Southern Gate, Chichester, West Sussex, PO19 8SQ, UK

For details of our global editorial offices, for customer services, and for information about how to apply for permission to reuse the copyright material in this book please see our website at www.wiley.com/wiley-blackwell.

The right of Gary W. Carter, Kevin W. Cook, and David W. Dorsey to be identified as the authors of this work has been asserted in accordance with the Copyright, Designs and Patents Act 1988.

Library of Congress Cataloging-in-Publication Data

Carter, Gary W.
    Career paths : charting courses to success for organizations and their employees / Gary W. Carter, Kevin W. Cook, and David W. Dorsey.
        p.   cm. – (Talent management essentials)
    Includes bibliographical references and index.
    ISBN 978-1-4051-7733-7 (hardcover : alk. paper) – ISBN 978-1-4051-7732-0 (pbk. : alk. paper)   1. Careers.   2. Industrial management.   3. Organizational effectiveness.   4. Success in business.   I. Cook, Kevin W.   II. Dorsey, David, 1952–   III. Title.
    HF5381.C3684 2009
    358.3′128–dc22

                                                                                    2008052088

A catalogue record for this book is available from the British Library.

Icon in Case Scenario boxes © Kathy Konkle / istockphoto.com

Icon in Career Path Guide box © Bubaone / istockphoto.com

Set in 10.5 on 12.5 pt Minion by Best-set Typesetter Ltd., Hong Kong
Printed and bound in Singapore by Fabulous Printers Pte Ltd

1   2009

Praise for *Career Paths*

"I like how Carter, Cook, and Dorsey have balanced the perspective and needs of the employee with the needs of the organization. They've provided a practical toolkit for practitioners, rooted in a strong conceptual model. I have looked at other sources on career paths in organizations, but this is the book I'd actually use to design a system."

Steven D. Ashworth, Ph.D, Manager – Human Resource Research & Analysis, Sempra Energy Utilities

"*Career Paths* is a straight-forward guide to strategic talent management, illustrating how to integrate recruitment/selection with training/development. It is highly recommended to human resource and employee development professionals who want to optimize their use of human resources."

Paul E. Spector, University of South Florida

"If you are, like me, a consultant who helps organizations develop and utilize their talent toward maximum performance; or a business leader trying to build a world-class organization with limited financial resources; or a Human Resources manager whose Generation Y employees are anxious to get ahead—you need to read this book. It clearly defines the 'why' and 'how' of using career path models as the foundation for a comprehensive talent management process. The ideas and methods defined in this book will help organizational leaders provide the structure to support employees' ambitions and will help employees understand exactly what they need to do to successfully manage their own careers. I am adding this book to my professional reference library."

Gena Cox, PhD, Managing Consultant, Human Capital Resource Center

Talent Management Essentials

Series Editor: Steven G. Rogelberg, Ph.D
Professor and Director Organizational Science, University of North Carolina – Charlotte

Senior Advisory Board:
- Eric Elder, Ph.D., Director, Talent Management, Corning Incorporated
- William H. Macey, Ph.D., Chief Executive Officer, Valtera Corporation
- Cindy McCauley, Ph.D., Senior Fellow, Center for Creative Leadership
- Elaine D. Pulakos, Ph.D., Chief Operating Officer, PDRI, a PreVisor Company
- Douglas H. Reynolds, Ph.D., Vice President, Assessment Technology, Development Dimensions International
- Ann Marie Ryan, Ph.D., Professor, Michigan State University
- Lise Saari, Ph.D., Director, Global Workforce Research, IBM
- John Scott, Ph.D., Vice President, Applied Psychological Techniques, Inc.
- Dean Stamoulis, Ph.D., Managing Director, Executive Assessment Practice Leader for the Americas, Russell Reynolds Associates

Special Features

Each volume contains a host of actual case studies, sample materials, tips, and cautionary notes. Issues pertaining to globalization, technology, and key executive points are highlighted throughout.

Titles in the Talent Management Essentials series:

Performance Management: A New Approach for Driving Business Results
Elaine D. Pulakos

Designing and Implementing Global Selection Systems
Ann Marie Ryan and Nancy T. Tippins

Designing Workplace Mentoring Programs: An Evidence-Based Approach
Tammy D. Allen, Lisa M. Finkelstein, and Mark L. Poteet

Career Paths: Charting Courses to Success for Organizations and Their Employees
Gary W. Carter, Kevin W. Cook, and David W. Dorsey

Mistreatment in the Workplace: Prevention and Resolution for Managers and Organizations
Julie B. Olson-Buchanan and Wendy R. Boswell

Developing Women Leaders: A Guide for Men and Women in Organizations
Anna Marie Valerio

Employee Engagement: Tools for Analysis, Practice, and Competitive Advantage
William H. Macey, Benjamin Schneider, Karen M. Barbera, and Scott A. Young

Online Recruiting and Selection: Innovations in Talent Acquisition
Douglas H. Reynolds and John Weiner

Senior Executive Assessment: A Key to Responsible Corporate Governance
Dean Stamoulis

Real Time Leadership Development
Paul R. Yost and Mary Mannion Plunkett

Contents

Series Editor's Preface   xi
Preface   xiii

Chapter 1   Introduction   1

What are Career Paths?   2
The Goal of This Book   19
Overview   21

**Chapter 2   A Conceptual Toolkit for Constructing
Career Paths**   23

Career Path Attributes   26
   Career Path Patterns   27
Outcomes   29
The Bottom Line   31

**Chapter 3   A Practical Toolkit for Constructing
Career Paths**   33

Sources and Methods   34
   Past   34
   Present   37
   Future   37
   A Note about the Special Role of Interviews and
     Focus Groups   38

How to Construct Career Paths   39
  Initial Steps   39
  Sequential List of Positions or Roles   47
  Qualifications   53
  Critical Developmental Experiences   54
  Competencies that are Accrued, Strengthened,
    or Required   56
  Career Success Factors   60
  Other Information   63
  Explicit Focus on Movement   64
  Promoting Alignment   64
  Assessment of Personal Attributes and Career Paths   64
Implementation Tips   65
The Bottom Line   67

Chapter 4   Integrating Career Paths into Talent
Management Systems I: Recruitment, Hiring, Retention,
Promotion, and Employee Development   69

Connecting the Employee to the Organization   69
Engaging the New Workforce   72
Recruitment and Hiring   73
Retention   80
Promotion   81
Development Planning and Execution   83
The Bottom Line   89

Chapter 5   Integrating Career Paths into Talent
Management Systems II: Strategic Workforce Planning,
the Early Identification and Development of Executive
Talent, and Succession Management   91

Keeping an Eye on the Big Picture   91
Strategic Workforce Planning   92
Identifying and Developing Early-Career,
    High-Potential Leadership Talent   95
  Who Are Our High Potentials?   95
  How Can We Develop (and Promote) Them Faster?   97
  Managing Communications Regarding High Potentials   98

Succession Management   99
  Evaluating Readiness for Promotion in
    the Context of Succession Management   101
  Methods for Evaluating Readiness   102
  Keeping Those "Not Yet Ready" on the Path(s)
    to Get There   102
The Bottom Line   105

**Chapter 6   Expanding Success Beyond the Individual
Organization – Industry and Economic Development
Perspectives   107**

Career Paths and the Industry Perspective   109
  Examples   110
  Differences between Industry Career Paths and
    Organizational Career Paths   116
Career Paths and the Economic Development Perspective   118
  Examples   120
  Differences between Career Paths Designed for
    Economic Development Purposes and
    Organizational Career Paths   124
Labor Market Analyses and Analyses of Cross-Occupation
    Requirements   125
  Labor Market Analyses   125
  Analyses of Requirements across Occupations   126
The Bottom Line   127

Chapter 7   Looking to the Future   129

Trend One – Demographic Trends   130
  Implications for Organizations   131
Trend Two – Technology   132
  Implications for Organizations   134
Trend Three – Globalization and Changing Organizational
    Structures   134
  Implications for Organizations   135
Trend Four – Defining Career Success   136
  Implications for Organizations   136
The Bottom Line   137

Career Path Resource List	139
Notes	143
References	147
Name Index	151
Subject Index	153

Series Editor's Preface

The *Talent Management Essentials* series presents state-of-the-art thinking on critical talent management topics ranging from global staffing, to career pathing, to engagement, to executive staffing, to performance management, to mentoring, to real-time leadership development. Authored by leading authorities and scholars on their respective topics, each volume offers state-of-the-art thinking and the epitome of evidence-based practice. These authors bring to their books an incredible wealth of experience working with small, large, public, and private organizations, as well as keen insights into the science and best practices associated with talent management.

Written succinctly and without superfluous "fluff," this series provides powerful and practical treatments of essential talent topics critical to maximizing individual and organizational health, well-being, and effectiveness. The books, taken together, provide a comprehensive and contemporary treatment of approaches, tools, and techniques associated with Talent Management. The goal of the series is to produce focused, prescriptive volumes that translate the data- and practice-based knowledge of organizational psychology, human resources management, and organizational behavior into practical, "how to" advice for dealing with cutting-edge organizational issues and problems.

Talent Management Essentials is a comprehensive, practitioner-oriented series of "best practices" for the busy solution-oriented manager, executive, HR leader, and consultant. And, in its application of evidence-based practice, this series will also appeal to professors, executive MBA students, and graduate students in Organizational Behavior, Human Resources Management, and I/O Psychology.

Steven Rogelberg

About the Series Editor

Steven G. Rogelberg Ph.D., is Professor and Director of Organizational Science a the University of North Carolina Charlotte. He is a prolific and nationally recognized scholar. Besides academic journals, his work has been featured in many popular press outlets (e.g., NPR, CBS News, *Chicago Tribune, LA Times, Wall Street Journal*). He is the current Editor of *Journal of Business and Psychology*. Besides his academic work, he founded and/or led three successful talent management consulting organizations/units.

Preface

The world has changed drastically, and these changes have had a profound impact on careers. Global competition, outsourcing, off-shoring, mergers, and acquisitions have impacted the employment relationship in fundamental ways, and societal and cultural changes have resulted in complex and highly varied career patterns.

Career paths have become increasingly varied, fluid, and emergent as people make career decisions within a highly dynamic organizational, societal, and global economic milieu. However, while career paths are increasingly complex and dynamic, they are by no means random, but rather can be understood and influenced. Indeed, this book demonstrates that in today's world, individuals and organizations *must* focus on career paths if they are to achieve their goals and maximize their success.

- Employees must assume increasing levels of responsibility for managing their careers, and organizations must offer meaningful career paths and flexible and alternative work arrangements to retain valued employees.
- The increasing need for an agile and ready workforce makes it important to attend more closely to the movement – and potential movement – of individuals within and among organizations and to the factors that make people suitable for jobs in diverse settings.
- It has become imperative for organizations to understand the capabilities of employees so that they can be optimally deployed, and to actively work with individuals to build their capabilities as they move through a series of roles.

The factors that have so dramatically changed career paths are the same factors that have made it imperative to focus on them. The well-worn paths of yesterday were easy to follow. In today's world, you must chart your course to success.

In this book, we demonstrate that career paths are the centerpiece of effective talent management systems, and highly useful mechanisms for realizing organizations' strategic human capital visions in today's world. We illustrate how career paths can be used to bring together individual career development, education and training, recruitment, hiring, retention, workforce planning, and succession management in a manner that ensures that individual and organizational needs and goals are met, and that enhances the potential of individuals and their effectiveness within organizations.

We also show, step by step, how to construct career paths, how to integrate career paths into a variety of human capital tools and processes, and how to use those paths to maximize individual and organizational potential. Practical advice and examples are provided throughout the book. We translate principles and concepts into concrete and practical career path development and implementation steps that business leaders, human resource professionals, industry representatives, educators, and training and development professionals can apply to maximize the success of individual employees, organizations, and industries.

Acknowledgments

Barbara Derwart who provided important insights into the economic development perspective on career paths. Roxanne Worden, Steve Gerety, and John Canery who provided assistance in preparing the figures and graphics for this book. Steven Rogelberg and an anonymous reviewer for their helpful comments and suggestions. Elaine Pulakos for inspiring us to write this book, but not for making it look easy. All of our colleagues at DDI and PDRI for their insights and expertise.

Chapter 1

Introduction

Everyone who participates in the world of work – including both paid and volunteer work – has a career path. In its simplest form, a career path is the sequence of work positions or roles that a person holds over the span of a lifetime.[1] Career paths can take as many different forms as there are people. They can be planned or unplanned. They can include a small number of positions or many positions. They can include upward, lateral, and downward moves (as defined by pay or status). They can be within a single organization (which is increasingly uncommon) or they can span several different organizations. They can be within a single industry or career field or they can span several related or unrelated industries or career fields.

Over the past three decades, career paths have become more varied and emergent as people make career decisions within an increasingly dynamic organizational, societal, and global economic environment. While individuals' career paths have always evolved over the course of their careers, the specific job movements of individuals have become more difficult to anticipate as the work environment has become increasingly complex and dynamic. This has led some to the conclusion that examining or specifying career paths is a futile exercise in today's world. This conclusion is dead wrong. In today's dynamic and complex economy, it is critical for the employees of your organization to have flexible career plans, to understand the factors – including the portfolios of skills – that will impact whether they achieve their career goals, and to pursue career development opportunities within your organization to make their dreams a reality. And, in the face of increasing global competition and increasing competition for top talent, it is more important than ever for your organization to understand and influence the increasingly complex and dynamic patterns of movement of people within and across organizations.

While most organizations focus a lot of attention on placing people into jobs to maximize organizational effectiveness (through employee selection, promotion, etc.), until very recently they tended to focus on the career paths of only a small number of "high potential" employees. (Fortunately, this situation is starting to change and recently we have seen a substantial increase in interest among leading organizations in the construction of career paths and their implementation as part of talent management systems.) A lack of focus on career paths is a serious mistake that results in significant missed opportunities for organizations and employees. In today's highly competitive world, organizations must focus on career paths if they are to succeed.

Consider the following questions:

1. I am a software engineer with 11 years' experience. I have Bachelors and Masters degrees in engineering. Will an M.B.A. benefit me at age 37?
2. The top candidates we recruit for our technical jobs keep asking what they can expect their career trajectory to be like five or ten years out. I know the outlook is bright, but I can't predict the specifics ten weeks out, let alone ten years out. What can we tell them?
3. Our company seems to be losing about 20% of our sales force just as they hit the two-year tenure mark. What is going on?
4. Some of our most talented employees are in the Non-agency Loan Securitization Division, but our business in that area has been decimated. Is there another place in our organization where we can utilize their skills?

Examining career paths will provide valuable information useful in answering these and many other questions that have important and direct implications for the success of your organization.

What Are Career Paths?

As noted earlier, in its simplest form a career path is the sequence of work positions or roles that a person holds over the span of a

Why Is It Important to Focus on Career Paths?

1. There is intense global competition in nearly every industry. Mergers and acquisitions have become increasingly common, and outsourcing and off-shoring are becoming more and more prevalent. As a result, the nature of the implicit employment contract has changed. Employees can no longer assume that their employer will have a place for them for many years, and organizations likewise cannot rely on a sense of loyalty to retain employees. Consequently, employees must assume increasing levels of responsibility for managing their careers, and organizations must offer meaningful career paths to retain talented employees.
2. With the changes in the economy, in organizations, and in the implicit employment contract, it has become increasingly important from individual, organizational, industry, and societal perspectives to have an agile, flexible, and mobile workforce that can thrive in a variety of situations, and that can be deployed to meet a variety of organizational needs. Thus, it is important to attend more closely to the movement – and potential movement – of individuals within and among organizations and to the factors that make individuals suitable for jobs in diverse settings.
3. Societal and cultural changes have resulted in more complex and varied career patterns. These changes include, for example, an increase in the number of families in which both adults work outside the home, an increase in the number of single-parent households, and an increase in the number of retirement-eligible persons who remain in the workforce in some capacity. To retain valued employees, organizations must understand the needs of employees and how jobs and job options can be shaped such that those needs are filled. Organizations must offer flexible and alternative work arrangements, and must make alternative career paths available to employees that work for them in the context of their life situations.
4. Increasingly, employees and organizations focus on the portfolio of skills that suit individuals for specific roles within an organization, and less on the "job" as traditionally defined. Effective organizations understand the portfolios of skills and other capabilities that drive their success, and how people possessing those portfolios of capabilities should be deployed at any given time to reap maximum benefits for the organization. These organizations also accurately anticipate which capabilities will be needed in the future, and where those capabilities will be needed. It has become more and more important for organizations to understand the capabilities of employees so that they can be optimally deployed, and to actively work with individuals to build their capabilities in a manner that maximizes value to the organization through a series of positions or roles.

lifetime. However, a fully developed career path should include much more than a list of positions or roles, and when building career paths you should consider much more than which positions to include and in what order. While the specific content should be driven by the objectives of the organization (business, government agency, industry association, educational institution) for which they are being developed, career paths typically include five fundamental components:

1. A sequential list of positions or roles. These are typically displayed in a diagram, making it easy to visualize each position or role as a node in a path. Frequently, the sequence of positions is shown in a "boxes and arrows" format, but a variety of visual formats can be used. Typically, a brief description of each position or role is also provided.
2. Qualifications (education, training, experience, licensure, and certification requirements) required or recommended at each node or each career stage.
3. Critical developmental experiences associated with each node or each career stage along the path. These may include, for example, formal training courses or specific stretch assignments that prepare a person for the next node, and on-the-job experiences.
4. Information about the competencies that are accrued, strengthened, or required at each node, at each career stage, or through each critical developmental experience (CDE). Different competencies are important at different career stages, and different levels of the same competency are required at different career stages.
5. Information about the sponsoring organization's perspective on, and management of, career success factors that are viewed as being of key importance. This may include, for example, the importance of depth versus breadth of expertise to career success, the importance of international assignments, the level of mobility that is desirable for the individual in a specific career and for the organization, and the type and patterns of movement that tend to lead to long-term career success (e.g., whether horizontal moves tend to lead to more promotion opportunities in the long run). This information – in terms of both content and presentation – is highly variable across organizations. While it is desirable to address it explicitly, it is frequently implicit in the paths that are constructed.

In addition to these five components, other information about the roles or positions comprising the paths is typically provided as part of a

Fundamental Components of Career Paths

1. Sequential list of positions or roles
2. Qualifications
3. Critical developmental experiences
4. Competencies that are accrued, strengthened, or required
5. Important career success factors

description of career paths. The nature of this information varies based on the purpose of the effort. For example, in cases in which career paths are being designed for use across organizations (e.g., for use by persons considering career options in an industry), information about salaries and anticipated growth rates in relevant occupations is typically provided.

Each of the five components described above is an integral part of a career path. However, what holds these components together and what makes the study of career paths different from any other aspect of human capital management is a focus on the movement of individuals over a significant period of time. The potential and promise of career paths lies in this movement, the dynamic aspect of careers and talent management.[2] Thus, the defining characteristic of career paths and of their use in organizations is an explicit focus on the movement of individuals over time. This focus on movement permeates all aspects of career paths and their use.

Defining Characteristic of Career Paths

The defining characteristic of career paths and their use in organizations is an explicit focus on the movement of individuals over time.

What are we really talking about here? Let's consider a hypothetical company – we'll call it Electronic Products Corporation, Incorporated (EPC, Inc.). In the pages that follow, we provide a sample career path guide for EPC, Inc. showing one of many possible ways to portray career path information. The guide shows potential sales, marketing, and products career paths in EPC, Inc. As you can see, the paths described in this guide include the five components described on page 4 and listed in the box "Fundamental Components of Career Paths." In addition, the guide provides basic information about how to interpret and use the career paths. We will refer to this sample career path guide throughout the book.

Sample Career Path Guide:
Sales, Marketing, and Products
Electronic Products Corporation, Inc.

Introduction

This Guide describes suggested Sales, Marketing, and Products career paths within Electronic Products Corporation, Inc. (EPC, Inc.). You can use these career paths and the information associated with them as resources in planning your career. They provide a "roadmap for success" that will help you to achieve your career goals.

The career paths, and the information associated with them, were developed by job experts – people in these positions – and executives from EPC, Inc. and reflect their recommendations. The information in this Guide will help you and our company succeed in the challenging, rewarding, and rapidly evolving marketplace. Use this information in conjunction with job descriptions and documented job requirements as you make decisions about positions, assignments, and developmental opportunities to pursue. You also should rely on your manager and/or mentor to help guide you along these paths.

What's in This Career Path Guide?

- A diagram showing potential Sales, Marketing, and Products career paths in EPC, Inc.
- A brief discussion of the qualifications needed at each level along the paths. Qualifications include education/certifications and required experience.
- Recommended developmental experiences associated with each level in the career paths that will prepare you for the next step in your career.
- Descriptions of key competencies that should be accrued or strengthened at each level along the paths.
- A brief discussion of career success factors identified through discussions with EPC, Inc. executives that will ensure that you – and the Corporation – are set up for success in light of our strategic direction and our rapidly changing business climate.

There are several important points that you should keep in mind as you review this Guide.

- While the career paths described are recommended by experts from the Corporation, these are not the only ways to succeed. There are many avenues to success in EPC, Inc. Regardless of the specific path that your career follows, you should constantly strive to strengthen the competencies that are relevant to your career goals.
- The critical developmental experiences described are not the only ones that contribute to career success. These experiences were identified specifically by job experts as being important at certain levels and therefore are represented as recommendations at the previous level to help you prepare for future roles. These recommendations are specified as requirements for success at the next level where appropriate.

There are many other experiences that also will help you to gain the skills and competencies needed to be successful within EPC, Inc.

- There is no guarantee that following a given path will lead to advancement to a specific level. Many factors beyond the control of individual employees impact promotions. However, pay attention to the qualifications, critical developmental experiences, and the related competencies that are presented with the career paths. Obtaining these qualifications, engaging in these experiences, and building these competencies will increase your chances of achieving your career aspirations.

Understanding the Career Paths

The career paths outline typical avenues for moving among and across jobs in ways that facilitate growth and career advancement. Job titles are shown in boxes. The arrows linking the boxes indicate the recommended moves among the jobs.

Understanding the Qualifications

The qualifications associated with each level are the recommended or required types/levels of education, training, and/or experience that, in general, are needed for successful performance at a given level. These are general qualifications recommendations or requirements (as indicated) – they do not represent the specific requirements for any given position. Qualifications requirements are established for specific positions and are highlighted in job announcements and position descriptions.

In general, the qualifications listed are cumulative. For example, a Bachelor's degree is listed as a typical requirement for Sales Coordinator positions. This qualification is not repeated at higher levels; a similar education requirement can be assumed for most subsequent positions unless a different requirement is specified.

Understanding the Critical Developmental Experiences

The critical developmental experiences are experiences that employees should acquire as they move through the career paths. The critical developmental experiences that are described in this document are those that job experts identified as required or particularly important to gain in preparing for career advancement. Each experience provides the opportunity to develop competencies that are important for success in EPC, Inc.

The critical developmental experiences are associated with a level in the organization, rather than with a specific position. These experiences, for the most part, are relevant across positions at a given level.

The experiences listed in this document are either recommended or required for advancement to the next level. Before you engage in a particular developmental experience, you should discuss the experience with your manager or mentor.

Continued

Individual Contributor

Sales Coordinator

Sales Representitive

Account Manager

Marketing Representitive

Channels Manager

Associate Product Manager

Product Manager

Corporate Marketing Rotation

CDEs

- Build Solid Foundation of Knowledge of EPC
- Complete Basic Financial Acumentraining
- Complete Sales Foundation Series Training
- Obtain Cross-functional Experience
- Obtain Cross-geography Experience

Competencies

- Focus on Customer
- Build Positive Working Relationships
- Business Acumen
- Market Focus
- Influencing Others
- Results Focus

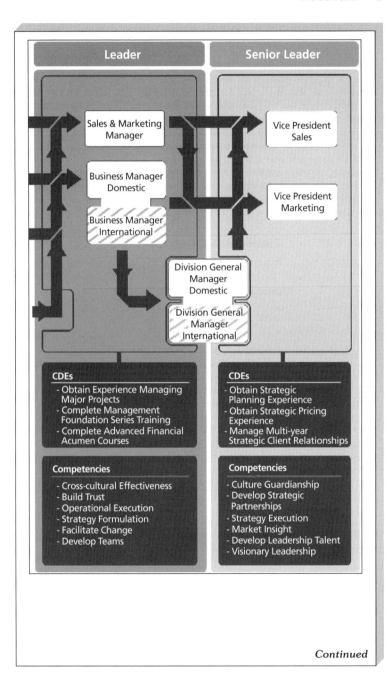

Leader	Senior Leader

Sales & Marketing Manager

Business Manager Domestic

Business Manager International

Vice President Sales

Vice President Marketing

Division General Manager Domestic

Division General Manager International

CDEs
- Obtain Experience Managing Major Projects
- Complete Management Foundation Series Training
- Complete Advanced Financial Acumen Courses

Competencies
- Cross-cultural Effectiveness
- Build Trust
- Operational Execution
- Strategy Formulation
- Facilitate Change
- Develop Teams

CDEs
- Obtain Strategic Planning Experience
- Obtain Strategic Pricing Experience
- Manage Multi-year Strategic Client Relationships

Competencies
- Culture Guardianship
- Develop Strategic Partnerships
- Strategy Execution
- Market Insight
- Develop Leadership Talent
- Visionary Leadership

Continued

Understanding the Competencies

The Competencies sections highlight key capabilities that should be accrued or strengthened at each level along the paths. While many competencies are important for success in each job, we've chosen to highlight only a few of those that are very important to develop at each level both to succeed at that level and to prepare you for success at subsequent levels in the organization. These highlighted competencies are most relevant across roles *within* each level and increase your likelihood of success across roles at the *next* level. The EPC, Inc. Individual Development Planning Guide contains comprehensive lists of important competencies for each position. Use that Guide, in conjunction with this document, as you think through your specific development needs and priorities.

Individual Contributor

Featured Titles – Sales Coordinator, Sales Representative, Marketing Representative, Associate Product Manager, Account Manager, Channels Manager, Product Manager

Qualifications

Most sales coordinator positions at this level require a Bachelor's degree and at least one year of relevant experience in a sales or marketing role, an administrative coordination role, or a sales coordination role. Preferably, the degree will be in a related field (e.g., Marketing, Business and Finance). Most other individual contributor positions require a Bachelor's degree and two to four years of experience in the preceding position, or in an equivalent position in another organization. For example, most sales representative positions require two to four years experience as a Sales Coordinator, or equivalent experience (as a Sales Coordinator or Sales Representative) in another organization.

Critical Developmental Experiences (Including Training)

Build solid foundation of knowledge of EPC, Inc. and its competitive position in the market
An understanding of our business and our competitive position in the marketplace is a key to success for all of our employees. The sooner this understanding is gained, the better. This experience involves engaging in any of a number of potential activities to build this understanding. These activities include, for example, taking the self-paced web course entitled "EPC 101," reading the company's annual report, and reviewing information about the company (including our organizational chart, and our annual Goals and Strategy document) available on the intranet.

Complete basic financial acumen training
- Company-wide, two-day training session (required for Leader candidacy)
- Function-specific training, if offered (recommended)

Complete Sales Foundation Series training
- "EPC-Sell!" two-day course focused on EPC products' features and benefits (required for Leader candidacy)
- "Why EPC?" – a three day, competitive differentiation session focused on market, customer segments, and key competitors (recommended)

Obtain cross-functional experience
- Work as part of a cross-functional project team or task force with a market, not internal, focus (required for Leader candidacy)
- Work in a role in another function at EPC (recommended)

Obtain cross-geography experience (all recommended)
- Ideal – live outside home geography for at least six months
- Helpful – work in a role with significant focus beyond home/current geography
- Key factor is to gain experience and exposure to cross-geography sales, marketing, and/or product areas

Competencies

Interpersonal
- Focus on the customer – make customers a primary focus of one's actions; meet customer needs; interact with customers in a fashion that can lead to a longer-term relationship
- Build positive working relationships – work effectively with others to support ongoing, productive relationships that facilitate accomplishment of goals

Business
- Business acumen – understand and apply financial and trend data to decisions and action planning
- Market focus – proactively seek market and industry data to inform decisions, action planning, and other efforts

Leadership (strongly recommended for Leader-level candidacy)
- Influencing others – use, and modify as needed, interaction style to gain agreement from others; create 'win–win' situations in dealings with others
- Results focus – set and pursue challenging, attainable goals for self and others; maintain and encourage a goal/outcome focus

Continued

Leader

Featured Titles – Corporate Marketing Rotation (Transitional Role), Sales and Marketing Manager, Business Manager

Qualifications

Most positions at this level require a strong cross-functional foundation. Leaders must have knowledge and experience across sales, marketing, and products. Leader candidates need not have held formal positions in each of the three functional areas but must have had some direct experience in each one (e.g., as part of a cross-functional team or initiative). Completing the Corporate Marketing Rotation is considered equivalent to having held an entry-level marketing position. Sales/Marketing and Business Manager positions require at least three years of experience in an Account, Channels, or Product Manager role at EPC. External candidates are considered for these roles but must complete foundational EPC training and development programs.

Critical Developmental Experiences (including training)

Obtain experience managing major projects
- Act as the lead project manager for two to three large projects with direct customer/market implications (required for Senior Leader candidacy)

Complete Management Foundation Series training
- Complete all MFS courses within specific timeframes (required for Senior Leader candidacy)
- Complete additional courses as approved by managing vice president (recommended)

Complete advanced financial acumen courses
- Complete one or more courses from advanced EPC curriculum – Global Finance, Anticipating the Economy, Managing Direct vs. Indirect Revenue Channels, Advanced Profitability Targets (recommended)

Competencies

Interpersonal
- Cross-cultural effectiveness – consider mores, norms and other factors when communicating and dealing with individuals from alternative cultural backgrounds
- Build trust – manage interactions with others in a way that shows respect and support and builds confidence in one's integrity

Business
- Operational execution – implement operational plans that support the attainment of goals within a broader strategy
- Strategy formulation – develop feasible, longer-term plans and courses of action to support strategic goals and the EPC mission

Leadership (strongly recommended for Senior Leader candidacy)
- Facilitate change – help individuals and groups understand and embrace change; minimize change resistance and focus on the "new state"
- Develop teams – apply appropriate leadership styles to build cohesive teams with clear goals, team charter and performance objectives

Senior Leader

Featured Titles – Division General Manager, Vice President of Sales, Vice President of Marketing

Qualifications

Division General Managers are required to have accrued substantial experience across the Sales, Marketing, and Product functions. Additionally, GM candidates must have completed all Management Foundation Series courses. Cross-cultural experience is highly preferred for this role. Vice Presidents must have completed all foundational *and* advanced/elective training within their area of specialty (i.e., Sales or Marketing). VP positions differ in their experience requirements according to geography. All positions require a strong background across functional areas. VPs must have held a leadership role within EPC for at least six years. Typical EPC minimum tenure for a new VP is eight years.

Critical Developmental Experiences (all recommended for continued advancement)

Obtain strategic planning experience
- Lead the planning of one or more strategic initiatives, including marketing, sales, product, and/or customer-focused programs
- Assume a significant role in EPC annual strategic business planning and priority setting

Obtain strategic pricing experience
- Develop and implement pricing for strategic market segments such as Channels, Enterprise, and Global segments

Manage multi-year strategic client relationships
- Manage at least two large, multi-year engagements with strategic clients, assuming accountability for overall success of the engagement

Competencies

Interpersonal
- Culture guardianship – always behave in a manner consistent with EPC's culture and values; encourage others to behave in a similar manner

Continued

- Develop strategic partnerships – use appropriate style and influence strategies to build and maintain relationships that facilitate the accomplishment of business goals

Business
- Strategy execution – translate strategic plans and initiatives into operational plans that can be executed across the organization
- Market insight – continually increase knowledge of market and business drivers; apply knowledge to create new opportunities

Leadership
- Develop leadership talent – identify and directly support individuals with potential to become future EPC leaders
- Visionary leadership – create and communicate a clear and compelling picture of the future for the organization; lead others in pursuit of the future state

International Leader and International Senior Leader

Featured Titles – Business Manager (International), Division General Manager (International)

Qualifications

International Leader and International Senior Leader roles include net new positions at EPC, Inc. Although we have similar positions in Canada and Mexico, those positions are part of North American Operations with job requirements that are very similar to leader roles in the United States. These new International roles also will have similar requirements initially but they will shift over time as our new international locations reach operating status.

At this time, the specified qualifications generally are the same as for their domestic counterparts; some geographies will have specific language proficiency requirements. One difference for these roles (including positions in these roles in Canada and Mexico) is that cross-cultural experience is required, rather than preferred. Prior experience does not need to have taken the form of an expatriate assignment but does require experience focused on a culture other than one's own. Candidates must also have completed the EPC cross-cultural awareness program. The CDEs differ for international roles, as noted below.

Critical Developmental Experiences (includes training)

(*Note*: Owing to space constraints, CDEs and competencies for International Leader/International Senior Leader roles are not shown on the career path diagram.)

Develop cross-cultural knowledge and awareness
- Complete cross-cultural awareness program (required of new International Leaders)
- Complete international rotation (recommended)
  - Initially within North America
  - Future opportunities in International Operations

Complete expatriate education program
- Combines individual and family-focused immersion orientation and education (required of new International Leaders)

Obtain global markets experience
- Gain direct exposure to markets outside one's own country through job rotation, project experience or cross-functional role (recommended)

Competencies

Competencies for International Leader roles are equivalent to parallel roles in North America, with the following additions:

Interpersonal
- Adaptability – manage one's style and approach to maintain effectiveness across varied business situations and interactions with others
- Persuasiveness – adapt communication and interaction style to influence the actions of others

Business
- Global acumen – understand and integrate varied sources of cultural, economic, market, industry and political data when setting strategic direction
- Resource allocation – effectively align and deploy resources to meet organizational goals

Leadership
- Influence – use influence strategies to communicate a position or desired outcomes to others in a manner that gains their support
- Impact – demonstrate a style consistent with the organizational culture and conveying confidence and leadership

Career Success Factors

At EPC, Inc., we understand that the success of our employees and the success of our company are one and the same – the Corporation cannot thrive unless our employees thrive. We offer rewarding, long-term careers with substantial potential for career growth, personal growth, and financial rewards.

Continued

Our executives have consistently stressed that passion, drive, and an ability to understand our customer's perspective are the most important factors leading to success at EPC, Inc. Those characteristics are important across the entire corporation. In addition to those factors, as part of the process of developing career paths, we looked at the applicability of three career success factors specific to the Sales, Marketing, and Products functions – breadth of knowledge and expertise, cross-geography experience, and the optimal length of time, on average, to stay in a position. These factors are discussed briefly below.

Breadth of knowledge and expertise
Broad knowledge of EPC, Inc. and its products and services, coupled with deep skills in one's core function (Sales, Marketing, Products) tends to characterize persons who make it to the Senior Leader level in the sales, marketing, and products functions. To achieve this breadth, we encourage gaining cross-functions experience, cross-geography experience, cross-market knowledge and expertise, and cross-channels knowledge and expertise at the Individual Contributor level. As shown on the career path diagram, we also encourage employees transitioning into leadership roles to pursue a corporate marketing rotation.

Cross-geography experience
EPC operates across many geographic regions in the United States. We also currently have operations in Canada and Mexico. Over the next five years we will become a truly global company with operations throughout the world. It always has been important for employees in the Sales, Marketing, and Products functions to gain cross-geography experience. This experience is becoming even more important as we expand our global reach. We encourage all employees to begin to gain this experience – by actively pursuing assignments and positions in different geographic regions within the United States and/or internationally – at the Individual Contributor level.

Optimal length of time in a position
Analyses of human resources data and executive opinions indicate that the optimal time to stay in a given position within the Sales, Marketing, and Products functions is, on average, three to four years. Most employees make lateral moves at both the Individual Contributor and Leader levels. This movement helps to ensure breadth of experience and skills, and continued professional development. However, there is no one "right" length of time to stay in a position – your specific individual circumstances and those of your business unit drive the optimal length of time for you to stay in a given position.

The box on pages 17 through 19 presents an EPC, Inc. overview and history. The overview briefly summarizes the history of the company, its current structure, market offerings, and culture/values, providing a context for understanding the implications of both external market factors and internal factors (e.g., company values, historical milestones) for career paths in EPC. The overview also summarizes current challenges and opportunities EPC is facing, and the decisions the senior leadership team has made to address these challenges and seize opportunities. As is the case with many organizations today, EPC has concluded that a significant focus on talent is needed to support its growth plans and overall strategic direction, including the development of career paths.

EPC, Inc. Company Overview and History

EPC Overview

- EPC, Inc. is a North American company that develops, manufactures, markets, and distributes mid-market consumer electronics
- EPC consists of several primary product areas, including:
  - televisions and digital video players/recorders
  - home and car audio equipment
  - cameras and camcorders
  - home office equipment
  - computer processor components
  - PC-based computer games
- Products are organized across three primary functions – Home, Office, and Entertainment
- Each Product function is responsible for its respective Research and Development, Manufacturing, Distribution, and Customer Service
- Marketing and Sales are currently centralized functions that operate across Products functions
- EPC's culture has three core values:
  1. Share the IDEA – inspire and encourage innovation and collaboration
  2. WOW the customer – retain customers through quality products and superior service
  3. Grow the RIGHT business – balance growth focus with high integrity practices

Continued

EPC History

Early years (1986–1992)
- Founded in 1986 by two entrepreneurs with electronics and engineering backgrounds – John Exeter and William Yosz
- Established operations with a single assembly facility in the Midwest
- Began with a regional focus only, quickly growing to prominence in the U.S. "heartland" and establishing distribution through Wal-Mart and Sam's Club in addition to its own channels
- Found early market success through quality products offered at a highly competitive price and supported with strong customer service
- Structured and managed like a more traditional, hierarchical organization with John as the conservative president of the organization and William as the dynamic driver of the sales and marketing functions

Growth years (1993–2002)
- Expanded across the entire United States including expansion of assembly capacity to meet rising production demands
  - opened seven new production facilities in the United States and one in Canada in 1998
- Consolidated position as one of the leaders in lower-cost consumer electronics products
- Competition and market pressure increased as foreign competitors increased their U.S.-based production and distribution, reducing their costs and holding prices relatively steady
- John passed away suddenly and William assumed control of the entire organization, revitalizing the entrepreneurial spirit of the company
- Industry competition spurred investment into new markets; rapid expansion of Sales and Marketing division under William's leadership
- EPC shifted to a matrix organization structure and operating model

Recent years (2003–present)
- Market share begins a slow but steady decline in the United States as the market becomes increasingly crowded and competitive
- Decision made to expand into Mexico in 2003 is enormously successful with innovative marketing campaign in Latin cultures
- Marketing function becomes much more influential
- Sales function expands greatly
- Product function continues to diversify with increased number of specializations
- U.S. Operations and North American Operations continue to emerge as parallel but increasingly distinct structures
- EPC entered the PC gaming market in 2003

Current Challenges and Opportunities

In September 2007, William Yosz convened his senior leadership team for a pivotal three-day meeting (referred to as "The Summit") to conduct a detailed review of EPC's strategic priorities and determine changes needed to regain the high growth trajectory of EPC. The following key challenges and opportunities were identified:

- Leadership bench is very thin with little internal talent ready to ascend to higher levels
- Significant internal challenges resulting from the emergence of political infighting and power struggles, turf wars, and unfocused strategies
- International competitors dramatically impacting market share and exponential growth needed to maintain market share
- EPC is having difficulty retaining young professionals – losing talent to new high-tech start-ups
- Product development and marketing coordination problematic at times
- Market trends and financial analyses confirm that emerging markets such as Brazil, Russia, and India represent greater growth opportunities than the North American market can provide

Future Outlook

As a result of The Summit, EPC made several strategic and operational decisions, most notably to rapidly and aggressively expand its international presence. International Operations has been formed as a parallel to the existing North American Operations. Both Operations comprise the global EPC, Inc.

The company plans to open twelve new operating locations outside North America within the next three years. Each of these locations will support EPC's full operational model – assembly, packaging, distribution, and service. Marketing, Sales, and Products functions also will be represented at each location. This planned expansion will affect every function and operation within the organization and draw heavily on the strong culture to ensure success.

Key execution points resulting from the decision include a focus on talent. EPC wants to address its growing leadership gap as quickly as possible. In addition to auditing existing talent to identify potential new leaders, the company also is revising its talent development strategies to support its new strategic direction.

The Goal of This Book

In this book, we demonstrate that career paths are the centerpiece of effective talent management systems, and highly useful mechanisms for realizing organizations' strategic human capital visions. We illustrate how career paths can be used to bring together individual career

Figure 1.1 Career Paths: The Centerpiece of Effective Talent Management Systems

development, education and training, recruitment, hiring, retention, workforce planning, and succession management in a manner that ensures that individual and organizational needs and goals are met, and that enhances the potential of individuals and their effectiveness within organizations.

The purpose of this book is to provide practical advice to business leaders, human resource professionals, industry representatives, educators, and training and development professionals about how to construct career paths, and how to use them to maximize individual and organizational potential. Our description of procedures for constructing career paths in Chapter 3 assumes that you are, or will be, conducting a project to develop career paths. However, even if your career path development efforts do not involve a formal project, it will still be useful to follow the basic steps outlined in this book. The approach offered here is both research-based and informed by career path development and implementation projects in many organizations. It focuses not only on the design and construction of career paths, but also on how you can use career paths to integrate a variety of human capital systems and processes to achieve valued business outcomes.

This book has three goals:

1. Show you how to construct career paths.
2. Demonstrate how career paths can be used to maximize individual and organizational potential.
3. Provide practical advice about how to use career paths to achieve important business outcomes by integrating them into a variety of human capital processes and systems.

Overview

The purpose of this book is to show you how your organization can design and use career paths. Chapters 2 and 3 provide conceptual and practical toolkits for constructing career paths. The conceptual toolkit presented in Chapter 2 includes a model showing facets of career paths and how they are used for a variety of purposes and at a variety of points across the span of a career (including organizational recruitment/entry, ongoing training and development, leader identification and development, strategic workforce planning, organizational retention and exit). The practical toolkit presented in Chapter 3 discusses information sources and methods for designing career paths, provides a step-by-step guide for you to use in constructing career paths that include the five career path components shown in the box "Fundamental Components of Career Paths" on page 5 and includes implementation tips that will ensure that the career paths you develop are useful – and used. It shows how you can use information about past career patterns, the present reality, and an organization's vision for the future to develop career paths, and describes how the purpose of the career path development effort drives the relative emphasis on past patterns, present reality, and future vision.

The next two chapters provide information about the practical uses of career paths for organizations, and include tools and tips for building comprehensive talent management systems with career paths as their centerpiece. Chapter 4 provides information about how career paths can be used by organizations for recruitment, selection, and promotion, how to improve employee retention using career paths, and how to integrate career paths into employee training and development systems. Chapter 5 describes how you can use career paths to enhance strategic workforce planning, the early identification and development of talent for the future, and succession management.

In Chapter 6 we look at career paths from a different angle, and describe the uses of career paths from the industry and economic development perspectives. Chapter 6 describes how you can use career paths to attract candidates to promising careers in industries and to align the efforts of partners from industry, government, and education to maximize the return on investment in regional education and economic development initiatives. In Chapter 6 we also discuss how analyses of occupational requirements can be used to build career paths that include multiple occupations.

The final chapter of the book, entitled "Looking to the Future," discusses the impact of four sets of trends on the career paths of the future. These include demographics, technology, globalization and changing organizational structures, and changing definitions of career success.

Chapter 2

A Conceptual Toolkit for Constructing Career Paths

In Chapter 1, we explained what career paths are and why they matter. In this chapter, we build upon the ideas presented in Chapter 1 to develop a conceptual model of career paths. In offering this model, our intent is neither to theorize nor to consolidate academic research on career paths. Instead, we strive to provide you with a rich conceptual "toolkit" that you can use to design and implement career paths in a way that makes the most sense for your organization.

A foundational model for our discussion is shown in Figure 2.1. As noted in Chapter 1, the main focus of this book is on the uses of career paths to maximize organizational success. However, as shown in Figure 2.1, career paths can also be viewed from the perspective of the individual and from the perspective of the industry.

How do or should organizations (meaning key leaders, stakeholders, members, etc.) think about career paths? One approach to tackling this question is to recognize that organizations are in a quest to win the proverbial "war for talent," and thus they seek to attract, recruit, and retain the best-fitting and most talented employees available. To achieve this goal, organizations operate human resource (HR) systems, and leading organizations integrate those systems and view them as components of the organization's overarching talent management approach. In this book, we show why this is the right perspective for today's organizations. Viewing HR systems as integrated components of an organization's overall talent management system puts the emphasis where it should be – on the holistic

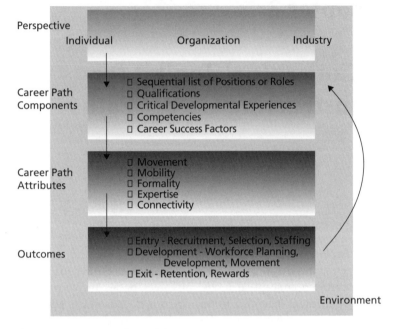

Figure 2.1 Career Path Model

management of careers. Thus, you can view recruiting, hiring, training and development, succession planning, compensation and benefits, mentoring, etc., as integrated components of the management
of careers – that is, getting, keeping, and developing talented individuals across useful career paths and career trajectories.

The following chapters focus on specific ways in which you can
describe, understand, and manage career paths. To set the stage for
these chapters, let's first consider what career paths mean from an
organizational perspective. First and foremost, career paths represent
the long-term value or equity proposition that organizations offer to
employees. Note that taking an equity perspective augments (but
should not replace) the traditional job/task-based approach to human
resources management.[1] From this perspective, career value propositions should be systematically designed, thoughtfully managed, and
effectively marketed for maximum impact. Ideally, modern career

value propositions would speak to a number of modern career trends that bring with them new challenges. These include an emphasis on personal interests and work–life balance, a focus on developing transferable skills, and an appeal to broader professional commitment that often co-occurs with decreased loyalty to a specific organization. When appropriately developed and communicated, such value propositions can have a positive impact on employee commitment, morale, loyalty, and satisfaction.

In addition to forming the basis of value propositions, career paths also represent a management leverage point; that is, career paths can affect the flow of human capital to and from various parts of an organization. This relates back to the focus of career paths on movement discussed in Chapter 1. Specifically, we are interested not just in static descriptions of jobs or career levels but also in understanding and possibly affecting movement. This idea is further explored in later chapters.

In addition to forming value propositions and serving as a potential management leverage point, career paths and talent management can serve as an organizing principle for investment in human capital development. By asking fundamental questions about the nature of the talent needed for different aspects of an organization's mission, priorities can be discerned regarding both short- and long-term development efforts. Moreover, development can be approached from a strategic point of view.

In our collective experience, where career paths and talent management have not been a strategic focus, haphazard, costly, inefficient, and ineffective training and development systems result – training and development staff attempt to close the latest skills gap that has caught an executive's attention rather than anticipating and meeting needs strategically. Ask yourself the following diagnostic question:

> How does my organization identify the appropriate level of investments and prioritize funding so that both short- and long-term training and development needs are addressed?

In other words, are investments made on the basis of immediate, first come first serve competency gaps, or on the basis of developing long-term human capital potential?

Career Path Attributes

How do you define a career path; what do they look like; how do career paths differ? In Chapter 1, we suggested that a career path is the sequence of work positions or roles that a person holds over the span of a lifetime, and we described the five fundamental components of career paths. In this section, we specify a set of career path attributes, which define the essence of career paths and relate directly to career success factors. Specifically, these factors impact both how individuals navigate career paths and how organizations and other stakeholders manage career paths.

In contrast to previous efforts, our goal is not to enumerate the factors that drive individual job and career choices. Instead, we seek to characterize career paths themselves, especially as they relate to larger talent management issues. The box below defines a set of career path attributes and highlights a few related questions about how such attributes influence the success of employees, organizations, and other stakeholders.

Overview of Career Path Attributes and Success Factor Questions

Career Path Attributes	Success Factor Questions
Movement: The degree to which movement within a career path is characterized by vertical or horizontal moves (e.g., linear, wheel patterns) Vertical ←——→ Horizontal	• What do moves within a career path facilitate in terms of acquiring new skills, knowledge, or other valued personal characteristics? • Are vertical or horizontal moves due to career management, development planning, or are they more idiosyncratic and unplanned? • What types of movement are most advantageous to a) individual success; b) organizational success? • Can generalizations be made about the types of movement that are most advantageous, or is it too idiosyncratic to make generalizations?

Career Path Attributes	Success Factor Questions
Mobility: The degree to which a path naturally promotes job or position change Mobile <———> Embedded	• Are individuals expected to move frequently, across either positions or jobs, and how is such movement facilitated or managed? • In general, how much movement is optimal for a) individual career success; b) organizational success?
Formality: The degree to which career paths are made explicit Formal <———> Informal	• Are career paths studied and understood? • Are career paths described by illustrative examples, a set roadmap, anecdotes, etc.? • Given the characteristics of the organization, occupation, or industry, does it make sense to develop set roadmaps, illustrative examples, or something in between?
Expertise: The degree to which specialized expertise is needed; variance in terms of breadth versus depth of expertise Broad <———> Narrow	• Are the expertise requirements of paths understood, and are developmental activities targeted to both short- and long-term development requirements? • Within a path, what is the relative value of breadth versus depth of expertise for a) individual career success; b) organizational success?
Connectivity: The degree to which a career path intersects with closely related paths or occupations Isolated <———> Connected	• To what extent are various career or occupational paths interconnected, and how might such connections be used for individual, organizational, or industry growth?

Career Path Patterns

To explore how these attributes describe career paths, consider the following generic career path patterns, which we label the specialist, generalist, and entrepreneur (see Figure 2.2).

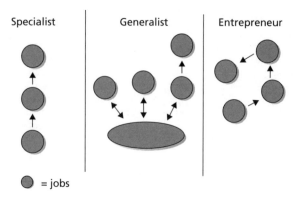

Figure 2.2 Career Path Patterns

   As shown in this figure, patterns of movement among career paths can be dramatically different. The specialist pattern is representative of careers involving adherence to a particular occupational field, often involving specialized education, knowledge and skills, and/or credentials that tie an individual to the field. Paths following this model might be characterized by relatively vertical moves (e.g., moving from Junior Engineer or Designer to Senior Engineer or Designer), fairly low mobility in terms of required job changes, often explicit/formal paths, a relatively high degree of reliance on technical and/or specialized expertise, and a moderate level of connectivity in terms of related fields (e.g., math, computer science, and engineering might all demonstrate connectivity).
   In contrast, a generalist career path pattern might be characterized by a large number of back-and-forth horizontal moves, allowing the individual to build a basic foundation of knowledge, skills, and expertise (think of a salesperson selling various products in various organizations, trying to find the "right" opportunity), a high degree of mobility, low formality, more general expertise, and moderate connectivity (e.g., sales might overlap with marketing, communications, etc.). Eventually, a generalist may move into a vertical path, for example, taking on a management or leadership role. Finally, a pattern such as that of the entrepreneur might be denoted by frequent movement, a high degree of mobility, little formality, diverse

expertise (depending on the domain of interest), and low connectivity. Paths such as that of the entrepreneur are generally characterized by a high degree of unpredictability. Note that these are just a few examples of career path patterns – numerous others exist.

So, how do the career path attributes and patterns described in this chapter help us to promote career and organizational success? By forcing us to think about how careers should be managed in an organization in light of the organization's mission and strategic direction. For example, should organizations encourage mobility? The answer depends on strategy. In growing organizations or units, embeddedness may be encouraged and mobility discouraged. In organizations or units on the decline, the organization may choose to tolerate increased external mobility.[2] Similarly, organizations may have various tolerances for different types and levels of movement, formality, expertise, etc. Later chapters focus explicitly on how organizations can manage career paths for maximum benefit.

Outcomes

All of the concepts and ideas about career paths, their attributes, and various perspectives are worth little attention if they cannot be tied to substantive and valued outcomes for your organization and its employees. Thus, in this section, we highlight briefly the last part of our conceptual model (think back to Figure 2.1), namely outcomes.

To elaborate a view of desired career outcomes, we focus on the uses of career paths and career information across different points in the employee "lifecycle" (i.e., entry, development, exit). The box overleaf highlights career outcomes in terms of a Practical Checklist for career path and talent management programs. Many of these important outcomes are explored in detail in subsequent chapters.

As shown in this box, career paths and talent management potentially touch all aspects of human capital and people management in organizations. It is for this reason that we suggested in Chapter 1 that career paths really should be the centerpiece of effective talent management systems. You can use the questions in the Overview of Career Path Attributes and Success Factor Questions box on page 30 to diagnose systems and programs in your organization. You may find the answers quite enlightening.

Career Path Outcomes

Outcomes	Practical Checklists
ENTRY Effectively bringing people into organizations and deploying them effectively Example programs: recruitment, selection, staffing, on-boarding, diversity policies	• Are messages about realistic career paths used in recruiting? • Are non-traditional talent pools identified and pursued? Are career path alternatives developed that would be appealing to such groups? • Are new hires provided with career counseling, mentoring, and career path guidance? • Does the organization have a clear and strategic policy regarding internal versus external sourcing? • Is career mobility assessed as a factor in evaluating a person's fit to the organization?
DEVELOPMENT Effectively training and developing individuals, optimizing fit between employee capabilities and needs and personal and professional goals Example programs: workforce planning, career planning and guidance, internal job markets, training and development, succession management, leader development, promotion/placement systems, performance management	• Are training and development programs, resources, and budgets focused on career development versus immediate training issues? • Are workforce planning models and systems used to assess talent pipelines, flow, and staffing to ensure progression along critical career paths? • Are individuals prepared early for critical positions (e.g., leadership positions), and are succession management and leader development programs integrated and in place? • Do promotion/advancement and performance management programs offer developmental and career-oriented feedback? • Are systems in place that deliver ongoing career planning advice as well as work–life balance options?
EXIT Effectively rewarding and recognizing employees so that valued employees are retained Example programs: reward and recognition programs, benefits, exit interviews, outplacement	• Are reward and recognition programs sufficient to facilitate retention of key talent? • Do occupational and compensation structures hinder career flexibility and adaptability? • Do reward programs promote immediate results to the detriment of long-term career development? • Are exit interviews or other methods used to assess exit points in key career paths? • Are outplacement services offered to promote external mobility, where needed?

The Bottom Line

In this chapter, we established a conceptual foundation for understanding the value of career paths in your organization and for designing and implementing an integrated talent management system with career paths as its centerpiece. However, looking at current organizational practices, you might ask: Why don't organizations do it? That is, why don't they even try to understand career paths, and why don't they take an integrated, career-based approach to talent management? There are multiple answers to this question. First, many organizational leaders view systematic talent management as too complicated and too future-oriented given the "what have you done for me lately" modern economic realities that organizations face. Second, there is substantial uncertainty about career development as a concept and practice.[3] Many human resource organizations are not equipped to develop and deliver sound talent management systems.

In addition, professionals such as us are to blame. We have convinced organizational practitioners that boundaryless careers are the norm, and employers and employees have internalized this message, believing that career paths are random and not worth planning. However, we feel strongly that such messages have been overstated, for several reasons. First, many individuals desire a sense of purpose and direction. Useful career guidance can provide such direction. Moreover, researchers have indicated that the traditional psychological contract may not be entirely dead.[4] Many individuals enter an organization with thoughts of staying for a number of years and seeking advancement and job movement during their tenure. Thus, a balanced perspective is needed. Although many organizations have flattened and/or blurred certain organizational boundaries, most organizations have not become fully "boundaryless." In addition, the idea that organizations in the past operated as highly hierarchical and bounded organizations, functioning in decidedly stable and predictable environments, is largely fiction. As pointed out by Yehuda Baruch,[5] organizational dynamics and uncertainty have been going on since the Roman Empire (if not earlier):

> We trained very hard, but it seemed that every time we were beginning
> to form up teams, we would be reorganized. I was to learn later in life

we tend to meet any new situation by re-organizing and a wonderful method it can be for creating the illusion of progress while producing confusion, inefficiency and demoralization. (Gaius Petronius, A.D. 66)

We believe that there is a solid business case to be made for understanding career paths and taking an integrated approach to talent management. While abilities and motivation are major determinants of job performance, opportunities also play a major role in determining effective performance – individuals misplaced in poor-fitting positions, jobs, and careers are unlikely to be productive. Thus, guiding individuals toward both present and future opportunities in a manner that optimizes fit represents an important value proposition for talent management systems. In the rest of this book, we discuss practical tools for developing career paths and integrating them into talent management systems. We end this chapter by providing you with one snapshot of an organization that has taken a systemic approach to talent management (see the box below).[6]

Case Scenario:
Integrated Career Management in the U.S. Navy: The Five Vector Model (5VM)

With all of the attributes, success factors, perspectives, and outcomes discussed above, one might wonder: is any type of integrated career management possible? The short answer is "yes." One recent example of an integrated career management system is the U.S. Navy's Five Vector Model (5VM). The 5VM provides sailors with opportunities to fulfill goals in both their professional and personal lives. At the heart of this initiative are five distinct areas of development, labeled "vectors" by the Navy. These vectors include: professional development, personal development, leadership, certifications and qualifications, and job performance. The 5VM is tied to a number of training, development, and career guidance systems and interventions that assist sailors in achieving in each of the five vectors.

For more information on the 5VM, see Hedge, Borman, & Bourne (2006).

Chapter 3

A Practical Toolkit for Constructing Career Paths

In this chapter, we show you how to construct career paths like the one shown in Chapter 1. We start by discussing sources of information and methods for developing career paths. These sources and methods can be grouped into three broad categories – past, present, and future. Each provides unique and valuable information. Ideally, you will use them together to obtain a comprehensive understanding of career paths in your organization.

Following this discussion, we show you exactly how to construct career paths using these sources and methods. We show, step by step, how to gather information about each of the fundamental career path components and how to use that information to construct career paths. In doing so, we refer several times to the sample career path guide shown in Chapter 1. We show you specifically how to develop career paths like the one shown in that example. Then, we briefly discuss the importance of focusing on movement when developing and using career paths, and of developing career paths that promote the alignment of the interests of the individual, the organizational unit, the organization, and (in some cases) the industry. Next, we discuss the role of the assessment of personal attributes in applying career paths. Finally, we provide practical implementation tips that will help you ensure that the career paths that you develop are actually used for their intended purposes and do not end up "sitting on the shelf."

The practical toolkit provided in this chapter is designed to be used hand-in-hand with the conceptual toolkit presented in Chapter

2, which showed how characteristics of an organization impact career paths in fundamental ways, and how career paths designed with those characteristics in mind can be used to great benefit for a variety of purposes. This chapter shows how to apply the conceptual toolkit when constructing career paths. Then, Chapters 4 and 5 show specifically how to apply the toolkits to integrate career path information into talent management systems. Together, Chapters 2 through 5 provide a comprehensive and practical approach for constructing career paths and integrating those paths into your organization's talent management system in a cohesive and coordinated way. Following this approach will enhance the success of your organization and its employees.

Sources and Methods

In this section, we discuss sources of information and methods for developing career paths. As noted previously, these sources can be grouped into three broad categories – past, present, and future. The purposes for which the paths are being developed drives the relative emphasis on what has worked in the past, the current reality, and the vision of the future. You will use these sources and apply these methods when you construct career paths using the specific process described in the "How to Construct Career Paths" section of this chapter.

Past

You can gather information about the past using either archival data – such as data available through human resources (HR) databases – or through interviews and focus groups. One of the advantages of using HR databases to gather information about career paths is that doing so allows you to test "folk theories" (i.e., untested beliefs held by many people) of career success in organizations to determine the accuracy of employee perceptions of what leads to success.

There are a variety of statistical indices and statistical modeling techniques that are used by organizations in workforce planning as tools to understand and manage hiring, deployment, promotions, and attrition. Similar techniques are used to examine labor supply, the demand for labor, and employee movement across entire occupations, industries, or sectors of the economy. You can use these indices and techniques to examine career paths in organizations, and to answer specific questions about the factors that are associated with promotion or attainment of a given organization level.

As described by Nalbantian et al.,[1] analyses of HR databases to examine workforce dynamics within a single organization can be labeled Internal Labor Market analyses, or ILM analyses. These analyses vary widely in their level of complexity. The simplest of these analyses can be used to show the percentage of people at various organizational levels, the percentage of people from a cohort who are promoted to a given level (e.g., 60% of the employees who complete the organization's senior executive development program are promoted to the rank of Vice President or above within three years), or the percentage of people in specific jobs, departments, or levels who move to other specific jobs, departments, or levels.

In describing their study of labor characteristics within an organization over a twenty-year period, Baker, Gibbs, and Holmstrom[2] discuss several analyses that can be conducted using HR databases to examine employee movement, career paths, and promotions. The diagram shown in Figure 3.1 provides a hypothetical example of a career path for an organization that is based on one of the techniques illustrated by Baker et al. In this example, the area of each circle represents the number of people in a given job over a specified period of time. The arrows show common movements between jobs and levels, and the percentages next to each arrow indicate the percentage of people in a job making that move. Diagrams such as this one can be developed to illustrate movement between specific job titles, or between job families or offices within an organization. In organizations in which there are many job titles and employees are not concentrated in a small number of those titles, it is typically more useful and feasible to examine firm-wide movement at the job family or office level, rather than the individual job title level. Then, analyses can be conducted at a more specific level to examine only those titles of particular interest at a given time (e.g., those of particular strategic importance over the next one to three years).

In addition to descriptive analyses showing the number or percentage of people at various levels or making various moves, more complex analyses – such as logistic regression analyses – can be conducted to identify specific factors that are associated with promotion

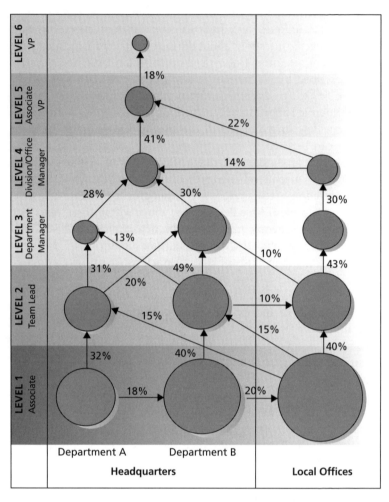

Figure 3.1 Career Path Diagram Showing Percentages of Incumbents Making Specific Moves

or specific job movements, and the relative importance of each of those factors. These analyses allow you to determine, for example, the extent to which education, performance ratings, time spent in training, etc., are associated with promotion, attainment of a specified organizational level, or a specific movement between one job or department and another. For a further description of ILM analysis including logistic regression techniques, see Nalbantian et al.[3]

Present

Information about the present state is gathered from incumbent employees using interviews, focus groups, and surveys. In most cases, input is gathered from employees at several levels of the organization. Typically, interviews and focus groups are used to identify the positions or roles comprising a path, recommended qualifications, critical developmental experiences, and career success factors. While this information can also be gathered using surveys or other structured questionnaires, interviews and focus groups are typically the preferred method for gathering this information because they allow for discussion and sharing of perspectives and information. In most cases, you can gather this information for one job or occupation in one or two half-day workshops.

In many cases, initial information about competencies that are accrued, strengthened, or required and information about qualifications is gathered using surveys. This information is then reviewed and refined during interviews and focus groups. Oftentimes, existing information sources can be used to derive draft lists of competencies and qualifications that are then refined through interviews and focus groups. We discuss some specific sources of this information later in this chapter.

Future

To build career paths based on the vision for the future, it is necessary to gather information about the strategic direction of the organization, and the implications of that direction for specific jobs, competency requirements, qualifications, and critical developmental experiences. You can obtain initial information by reviewing your organization's overall strategic plan and its human capital strategic plan (if such a plan exists). In addition, you can use surveys to gather information about anticipated changes in performance expectations (e.g., "we will need more leaders who can help us penetrate new global markets"). However, a review of plans and survey results is not sufficient to design future-focused career paths. It is critical to meet with people who understand the organization's vision for the future, and the implications of that vision for career paths. Typically those people are executives and high-level managers who have a role in developing and implementing the organization's human capital strategy. Thus, future-focused career path interviews and focus groups should include those executives and managers.

A Note about the Special Role of Interviews and Focus Groups

As noted in this section, there are many methods available to you for gathering career path information. However, interviews and/or workshops are central information gathering methods in almost all career path projects. There is simply no better or more efficient way to gather information about some of the career path components, such as information about critical developmental experiences. Typi-

---

Criteria for Selecting Career Path Interview/ Workshop Participants

- Collectively, have an in-depth understanding of all of the target jobs or occupations.
- Collectively, can address all levels of the career paths; to do this, some participants should be at or above the highest level represented on the paths.
- If paths are being designed for a single organization – collectively, have in-depth knowledge of the target jobs in different locations and business units.
- If paths are being designed for an occupation or industry and not a single organization – collectively, have in-depth knowledge of the target jobs in a variety of organizations.
- If paths are being designed for a single organization – have adequate tenure in the organization (typically at least two years).
- If future-focused career paths are being developed – includes people who understand the organization's strategic vision and the implications of that vision for career paths (typically executives and high-level managers).
- To extent possible, includes a demographically diverse set of participants (age, gender, race).
- Are available to participate in interviews or workshops during the project period.

cally, individual interviews are conducted to gather initial information, and then workshops are conducted. However, in cases in which high-level executives are participating, it is often necessary to conduct individual interviews with them due to schedule constraints and due to a common hesitancy among employees to speak up during workshops when a high-level executive is present (particularly in cases in which they disagree with the executive). Criteria for selecting persons for career path interviews and workshops are provided in the box on page 38.

In most cases, all of these criteria except the first can be met with a single group of six to ten interview or workshop participants. (It is usually necessary to have different sets of participants for different jobs or occupations, unless the jobs or occupations are interrelated or are in the same organizational unit.)

How to Construct Career Paths

In this section, we show you exactly how to construct career paths using the sources and methods we discussed in the previous section. First, we describe five initial steps that you should take. Then, we discuss how to construct career paths containing each of the fundamental career path components described in Chapter 1. Our description assumes that you are conducting a project to develop or update career paths. However, even if your career path effort is not envisioned as a formal project, it is still useful to follow the process described in this section.

Initial Steps

1. Identify the stakeholders At the outset of a career path project, identify the stakeholders for your project. Think about who initiated the project, who can benefit from it, and who has the power to make the project a success or a failure. These people will include the organization's main point of contact for the project, or POC. If you are the person initiating the project in your organization and you will be the point person for the project, then you are the POC. In projects conducted in Federal Government organizations using contractors, this person is usually the Contracting Officer's Technical Representative, or COTR. Stakeholders also include employees in jobs to be addressed by the career paths, and (in many organizations) union representatives. Importantly, stakeholders also include organizational decision-makers. It is very important to gain the support of high-level organizational officials early in any career path project.

2. Ask the right questions Career path tools – like all human capital tools – should be purpose driven. The purposes for which career paths are being designed should determine the sources of information used to gather career path information, the methods used to develop career paths, and the focus and content of career paths. Below we present three key questions about the purposes for developing career paths, and discuss the implications of the answer to each of those questions for career path information sources, development methods, focus, and content. Answering these questions before you begin constructing career paths will help to ensure that the career paths you design are useful – and used.

• Will the emphasis be on maximizing outcomes for the individual, the business unit, the organization as a whole, or the industry? The answer to this question influences the content of career paths. For example, if the emphasis is on maximizing outcomes for the organization, certain positions or assignments for which there are many openings and a dearth of candidates may be included in recommended paths that would not be included if the paths were being designed primarily to maximize outcomes for individuals. Similarly, if the emphasis is on maximizing outcomes for the organization as a whole, jobs in various parts of the organization may be included that would not be included if the emphasis was on maximizing outcomes for a particular business unit. Of course, in some cases there may be an equal emphasis on two, three, or even all four of these entities. For example, the career paths built for Electronic Products Corporation that are shown in Chapter 1 were designed to maximize outcomes for individual employees, the Sales, Marketing, and Products functions, and the organization as a whole.

There is usually substantial overlap between the interests of individuals, business units, and organizations in the career path arena. However, they are typically not perfectly aligned from the perspective of either employee perceptions or reality. For example, transfers of high-potential employees between business units may help the organization as a whole, but may hurt a particular business unit. As another example, in some organizations frequent movement among positions may be beneficial to individual careers, but frequent movement of large numbers of employees may be highly detrimental to organizational performance. Even if frequent movement is not actually beneficial to individual careers, it may be perceived as such by employees, leading to frequent, unnecessary, and disruptive movement. An important benefit of systematically examining career paths – including promotion rate information – is that doing so allows you to identify "folk theories" about what it takes to succeed in the organization, and to determine the extent to which those theories reflect reality.

While complete alignment may not be practical in many organizations, serious misalignment points to a need to take action to ensure that individuals are rewarded for career decisions that are in the best interest of the organization. This may include, for example, changing transfer and promotion policies and placing more emphasis on strategic workforce planning. Career path projects provide the opportunity to explore the degree of alignment between the interests of individuals, business units, organizations, and industries in the movement of employees, and to identify ways to bring the interests of these entities into closer alignment.

- Is the focus on the past or the present (understanding "tried and true" paths to success) or on the future (driving organizational change)? If the focus of the project is on helping individuals understand the proven paths to success in the organization, then the most useful sources of data will be sources that provide information about the past (such as human resource databases providing information about employee movement over time) and the present (such as workshops with employees who provide information about typical career paths). If the focus is on driving organizational change, then the most useful sources of data will be sources that provide projections about the future or well-grounded visions of the future of the organization and the industry. These sources include interviews or workshops with corporate "visionaries" who understand and impact corporate strategy and who understand current and anticipated industry trends and the likely impact of those trends on the organization. The focus of the career paths built for EPC, Inc. was on both the present (what works now) and the future (what is needed for the future in light of an anticipated international expansion).

• What are the main reasons the career paths are being developed? In Chapter 1 we stressed the role of career paths as centerpieces of effective talent management systems, and noted that career paths can be used to bring together individual career development, education and training, recruitment, hiring, retention, workforce planning, and succession management. Typically, however, there is an emphasis on one or two of these related systems in the development of career paths. This emphasis impacts the information that is included in career paths. For example, if the career paths are being developed primarily for employee development or education and training purposes, then detailed competency information should be included, and the career paths should link directly to – and in some cases may even incorporate – training and development roadmaps. If the career paths are being developed mainly for workforce planning or succession management purposes, information about the anticipated numbers of employees needed at each node along the career paths is often included. Moreover, if the paths are being developed for succession management purposes, they may be designed for a relatively small subset of high-potential employees and may therefore include assignments or positions for which there are few openings. Such assignments or positions would not be included in paths designed to guide large numbers of employees. While the EPC, Inc. career paths were designed to support several human resource systems, the main focuses were on workforce planning and succession management as the organization prepared for rapid international expansion.

  If your organization is developing career paths primarily to support recruitment, hiring, promotion, retention, or employee development programs, refer to Chapter 4 for a detailed look at how you can integrate career paths into those programs. If the emphasis of your effort is on strategic workforce planning, succession management, or high-potential talent programs, read Chapter 5 to learn how you can integrate career paths into those programs.

Case Scenario:
Driving Strategic Change at the Securities and Exchange Commission

The mission of the U.S. Securities and Exchange Commission (SEC) is to protect investors, maintain fair, orderly, and efficient markets, and facilitate capital formation. The success of the SEC in achieving this critical mission in an expanding and increasingly complex global securities environment will depend to a significant extent on whether it can continue to attract and retain a highly skilled workforce, and whether it can deploy and utilize that workforce in an effective and flexible manner as new challenges arise. Recognizing this, the SEC undertook an initiative to transform its human resources organization from a transaction-based organization to one that would provide strategic human resource consulting services to the agency's operational units. SEC's leadership understood that to do this, HR staff would need additional competencies, new roles would need to be developed (including, for example, roles for HR staff embedded in operational units) and higher-level HR positions would need to be created to attract and retain highly skilled HR professionals.

At the same time it was making organizational changes to accommodate the new direction, SEC identified future-focused career paths for its human resources organization. The career path project team (which included both contractors and internal staff) first met with executives to gain an understanding of the vision for the future. Based on information gathered in that meeting, the organization's human capital strategic plan, and information about current opportunities and competency requirements, the team prepared draft documents depicting career paths in the transformed HR organization. The draft career path documents provided visual depictions of career paths, described critical developmental experiences at each career step, and delineated the competencies that are accrued or strengthened at each career step. The team then met with HR staff, including managers who understood the vision for the transformed organization, and refined the draft career paths. The career paths are being used to help HR staff understand the vision for the future of the SEC's HR organization, and to help them identify and pursue career development options that will allow them to achieve success in the transformed organization.

In this case the interests of *individual employees*, *the business unit*, and the *organization as a whole* were emphasized equally. The focus of the effort was on *driving organizational change*, and the paths were designed mainly for *employee development* purposes.

Case Scenario:

Attracting People to Careers in the Home Building Industry

The Home Builders Institute (HBI) is the workforce development arm of the National Association of Home Builders. HBI is dedicated to promoting the home building industry and career opportunities within that industry so that its members will have an adequate professional, technical, and skilled-trades workforce to build and maintain America's homes. HBI launched the Careers Campaign to improve the home building industry's image, to promote home building careers, and to encourage people to consider home building as a career option. The Careers Campaign, with a theme of "Make It Happen," provides information about the home building industry to members, educators, students, parents, and others through the web (www.buildingcareers.org), print materials (including a brochure and poster), and a video.

As part of this campaign, HBI developed a career path diagram and associated documents providing information about jobs and career steps (including education and experience requirements) in the home building industry. Sources used in developing the career path diagram and the associated documents included America's Career InfoNet (www.acinet. org/acinet/; a web-based resource sponsored by the U.S. Department of Labor), and the *Occupational Outlook Handbook*.

In this case the emphasis was on maximizing outcomes for *individual employees* and the industry, the focus of the effort was on representing *current career opportunities*, and the paths were designed to *attract qualified individuals to the industry*.

Table 3.1 summarizes the implications of each of the three questions discussed in this section for information sources, development methods, and the focus and content of career paths. In practice (as was the case in our EPC, Inc. example), the answer to these questions is frequently "both" or "several." (For example, the focus may be both on understanding successful paths in the past and on driving strategic change rather than one or the other.) Nonetheless, carefully considering these questions and the implications of them at the outset of a career path project will help you to develop career paths that make the most sense for your organization.

3. Identify the target jobs Decide upon a target set of jobs, occupations, roles, and/or organizational levels upon which the career paths will focus. While in some cases this is obvious (e.g., the goal is to

Table 3.1 Practical implications of questions for career paths

Question	Primary Information Source	Development Methods	Focus and Content
Whose interests will be emphasized?			
Individuals	Various	Various	Stress what is best for individual career advancement
Organization	Various, but specifically includes managers/ executives	Various, but includes interviews/ workshops with managers/ executives	Stress what is best for organiza-tional success
What is the focus?			
On the past or present – Under-standing "tried and true"	HR databases, managers	Analyses of HR databases, workshops with long-tenured managers	Proven paths to success in past and/ or perceptions of what works today
On the future – Driving strategic change	Executives	Interviews/ workshops with executives	Vision of what will lead to success in future
What is the main reason for path design?			
Workforce development	Various; often includes detailed competency survey	Various	Includes detailed competency information; focus on large percentage of employees
Succession management	Various, but specifically includes managers/ executives	Various, but includes interviews/ workshops with managers/ executives	May focus on relatively small subset of employees; if so, may describe opportunities available to relatively few employees

develop career paths for a specific set of human resources jobs in a Federal Government organization), in other cases it is not (e.g., in an organization in which there are hundreds of job titles and there is not clear direction from the POC regarding where to focus initially, or in an organization in which movement through positions is based explicitly on skill portfolios that are not linked to job titles). This decision can be based on many different considerations, including, for example, which jobs are the most populous in the organization, which jobs are considered most critical to the success of the organization, or a specific issue that has been identified with regard to a particular set of jobs – such as high turnover stemming from a perceived lack of opportunity in a critical job or at a certain level in the organization. Ask yourself or your stakeholders: "Given the purposes for which we are developing career paths, what set of jobs, occupations, roles, and/or levels does it make the most sense to target?"

In the EPC, Inc. example provided in Chapter 1, corporate executives identified the Sales, Marketing, and Products functions as being key both to the organization's current success and to the anticipated rapid expansion of the business. Thus, a decision was made to target key jobs in those interrelated functions.

4. Develop a project plan Develop a project plan that describes the purpose of the career path project, identifies the target jobs, outlines the main steps comprising the project, provides a timeline for conducting the project, and clearly specifies who will do what during the project. Depending upon the size and complexity of the project, project plans can be brief and simple documents or lengthy documents that include an in-depth description of project contingencies, link to a work breakdown structure (WBS), etc. In almost all cases, a simple project plan is sufficient and preferable in career path projects. There are many resources available that describe how to develop project plans, including books and courses available from the Project Management Institute.

5. Develop a communication plan To ensure project success, develop a plan for communicating with stakeholders. Such a plan need not be lengthy or complex; in smaller projects it may simply consist of a few bullet points that are included as part of the project plan. However, it should be carefully thought through. The communication plan describes how you will communicate with project stakeholders –

including interview and workshop participants, employees in jobs addressed by the career paths, union representatives, and organizational decision-makers. For example, it is invariably very helpful for a high-level official in the workshop participants' direct chain of command to voice his or her support for the project during meetings and via e-mails or memos. We typically encourage the official to send an e-mail to workshop participants a week or so prior to the time that a workshop invitation is sent out, explaining the purpose of the project and communicating his or her support for the effort. Simple e-mails of this nature can go a long way toward ensuring the participation and support of job experts and, ultimately, project success.

Once you have completed these initial steps, you are ready to begin to construct career paths. In Chapter 1, we stated that career paths typically contain five fundamental components: 1) a sequential list of positions or roles; 2) required or recommended qualifications at each node; 3) critical developmental experiences associated with each node; 4) the competencies that are accrued, strengthened, or required at each node or through each critical developmental experience; and 5) information about the sponsoring organization's perspective on career success factors. The sample career paths shown in Chapter 1 include each of these five components. In addition, we noted that other information about the roles or positions comprising a career path (such as information about salaries and anticipated growth rates in relevant occupations) is sometimes provided as part of a description of career paths. We will now show you how to construct career paths containing these components.

Sequential List of Positions or Roles

A sequential series of positions or roles displayed visually using a diagram (often a "boxes and arrows" diagram) is the most fundamental component of a career path, and it is what most people think of when they think of a career path. An example of one such diagram is included in the sample Career Path Guide shown in Chapter 1. A second example, using a somewhat different format, is provided in Figure 3.2. (The career path shown in Figure 3.2 is for illustrative purposes only. It was derived in part from information on the National Retail Federation website [www.nrf.org].) Analyses of human resources data can be used to identify career paths that have been successful in the past (i.e., "tried and true" career paths).

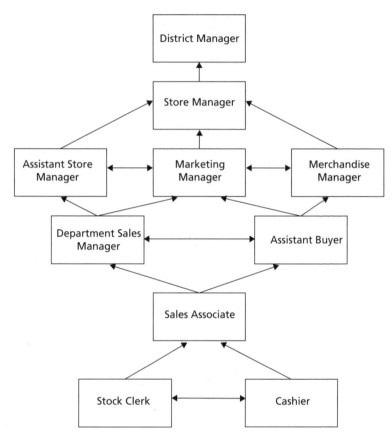

Figure 3.2 Example Career Path Diagram for the Retail Industry

Interviews and workshops are typically used to identify current career paths, and career paths that reflect and promote the organization's vision for the future.

As a starting point in developing a list of jobs or occupations comprising a career path, gather information about the relevant jobs or occupations. This information may include, for example, position descriptions and information from the U.S. Department of Labor's O*NET system (http://online.onetcenter.org/). Educate yourself about the target jobs, and think about how the target jobs or positions may fit together into a career path. This base of knowledge is important regardless of the specific methods you are using to develop the career paths. In developing the EPC, Inc. career paths shown in Chapter 1, the developers started by reviewing position descriptions and training materials relevant to the target jobs.

Analyses of human resources data As discussed previously, HR data-bases can be valuable sources of information about career paths that have historically been popular or fruitful. In the past, it was very difficult to utilize human resources data to examine career paths because these data were kept in paper files. Now, however, the vast majority of organizations maintain human resources data in electronic form, and most medium-size and large organizations maintain these data in an organized and accessible form in a human resource information system, or HRIS. Moreover, many organizations have been using these systems for a number of years. Consequently, data are now frequently available in electronic form over a long enough period of time to examine the career movement and progression of employees, even if old paper records were not transferred to these systems. As a result, it is now much more feasible than it was in the past to obtain and analyze human resources data to identify career paths.

In general, we do not advise conducting analyses of information in HR databases on your own unless you have data analysis training and experience. Many large organizations have staff within their human resources departments who routinely conduct analyses (such as workforce modeling analyses) of data in human resources databases. These people can be excellent sources of information or assistance in analyzing human resources data to derive career path information.

Regardless of who will be conducting the analyses, an important first step in using human resources data to examine career paths within an organization is to find out what data are available and the form in which those data are available. Talk with the relevant people in your human resources department to determine, for example, the specific information that is available in the databases, the form in which these data are kept, and the period of time for which such data are available electronically. Ask specific questions about the data to determine how feasible it would be to track the movements of employees through titles or levels over time. The answers to these questions will help you to determine the potential usefulness of human resources databases in deriving career path information.

Interviews and workshops If you are identifying a list of positions or roles comprising the career paths using interviews and workshops, start by conducting initial interviews with a few people who understand the purpose of the project, and who are knowledgeable about the target jobs. These people will include, but should not be limited to, the POC. In the EPC, Inc. example, the consultants on the project started by interviewing the POC (a representative from the HR department) and an operations executive representing each of the three target functions (Sales, Marketing, Products). Work with these people to develop initial draft career paths to use as a starting point in later interviews or workshops with job experts. In addition to working with these people to construct initial draft sequential lists of positions or roles, you should discuss the sponsoring organization's perspective on career success factors with them. This step is described later in this chapter. In addition, if the career paths are to be future focused, use these initial interviews to gather information about the organization's strategic direction and the implications of that direction for the target jobs. Because one of the main reasons for developing the EPC, Inc. career paths was to support the anticipated international expansion of the company, the consultants focused a substantial portion of the initial interviews on gathering information about the company's strategic direction and the implications of that direction for the target sales, marketing, and products jobs. Depending upon how knowledgeable the persons you are interviewing are regarding the specific details of the target jobs, you may also be able to gather initial information about other components of the career paths from these people. It is best to use an informal approach during these initial interviews. In the EPC, Inc. project, the consultants started by simply asking: "In light of the purposes of the project, what is a reasonable career path for a person in the [sales, marketing, products] function?" Use a flipchart to draw the career paths as you discuss them. Remember, the purpose here is not to develop the final paths; it is simply to provide a starting point for later interviews and workshops.

Use the information from these initial interviews, in conjunction with other information you have gathered about the jobs (e.g., from position descriptions), to construct visual depictions of career paths for the target jobs.

In addition to gathering initial information regarding the sequence of positions comprising career paths during these interviews, you can also use these interviews as an opportunity to share and refine the team's vision of the end product. In the EPC, Inc. case, for example, the consultants had originally planned to identify distinct qualifications, critical developmental experiences, and competencies for each job represented in the paths, and this is what was reflected in the project plan. During the initial interviews and through a series of discussions with the POC, however, it became apparent that there was a great deal of overlap in each of these areas among jobs within a level, even among jobs in different functions. Moreover, it became clear that EPC, Inc. saw this overlap as a corporate strength because it made cross-functional moves easy and largely prevented functional "silos" from forming. In addition, the POC stressed the importance of producing a simple and brief career path document even if some information about important qualifications, experiences, and competencies that may be specific to a given job had to be sacrificed. In light of these factors, the project team decided to present information about qualifications, critical developmental experiences, and competencies by level rather than by job. This change illustrates the importance of the cardinal rule in any career path development project: Be flexible!

Next, conduct more formal interviews or workshops. You will gather information about several career path components, including the positions or roles comprising the paths, during these interviews or workshops. Use the criteria provided in the box "Criteria for Selecting Career Path Interview/Workshop Participants" to select participants for these interviews or workshops. As noted previously, in the EPC, Inc. example, the three target functions (Sales, Marketing, Products) were seen as highly interrelated. Therefore, instead of holding separate focus groups with representatives of each of these functions and developing distinct career paths for each of them, three focus groups were held that each included two to three managers representing each of the three functions (a total of six to nine representatives in each focus group), resulting in an integrated set of career paths cutting across the three functions.

If the career paths are to be future focused, start by discussing the organization's strategic direction with the participants and explain that the paths should reflect this direction. Then, show a visual depiction of a career path you plan to discuss with them. Stress to the participants that the initial draft paths are just a starting point, and that they may need to be revised extensively.

Questions that can be used to solicit information about the positions or roles comprising the career paths are shown in the box below. You should choose specific questions based on the goals of your project. For example, if the goal of the project is to drive strategic change, you should focus on questions regarding the paths of the future rather than on questions about typical career paths. Depending upon the scope and focus of the project, you may want to include questions about career paths that cross organizational units or occupations. However, be clear about the parameters of the project and of the jobs/roles being addressed in a particular interview or workshop – theoretically, a career path diagram could be developed that includes all positions or roles in an organization.

Questions to Solicit Information about Positions or Roles Comprising Career Paths

- What are the positions or roles that comprise a typical career path of a person in this job/occupation?
- What series of positions or roles should a person hold if his or her goal is to make it to the x level in this job/occupation?
- Are any typical career paths missing from the initial draft model?
- Are any of the draft paths inaccurate or uncommon?
- How does the typical career path of today differ from the career path of the future, given the organization's strategic direction?
- What positions or roles will comprise a successful career path in the future?
- How should the initial draft career paths be changed to reflect the organization's strategic direction?
- What positions/roles/jobs allow one to gain the experience and competencies important at higher levels, and how do they fit together to form a career path?
- What positions/roles/jobs tend to lead to promotions, and how do they fit together to form a career path?
- Do the initial draft paths capture both realistic paths within this occupation, and realistic cross-occupation paths? If not, what paths are missing?
- Are there realistic or typical paths that cut across units or departments within the organization? If so, what are those paths?

Qualifications

While the specific information about qualifications included in the career paths will vary depending upon the purposes for which the paths are being developed and the intended audience, it is generally useful to include information about required and/or recommended education, training, experience, licenses, and certifications. (Experience, when included as part of this career path component, typically refers either to years of experience performing a particular type of job or to general experience recommendations [e.g., "experience assisting managers with compensation and benefits issues"]. Specific developmental experiences are captured in the Critical Developmental Experiences career path component.)

The qualifications presented in the EPC Career Path Guide are established qualifications in EPC, Inc. obtained from the company's HR department. These qualifications were reviewed during the workshops to determine whether they were suitable for use in the career paths in light of the fact that they were developed to represent current requirements, and position duties were likely to change somewhat during the anticipated period of rapid international expansion. Workshop participants agreed that, while there were some additional qualifications for specific positions that weren't reflected in the qualifications provided for each level, the general qualifications provided by the HR department were appropriate at the time the workshops were conducted and would continue to be appropriate in the near future. (As noted in the EPC Career Path Guide in the description of qualifications for the International Leader and International Senior Leader roles, qualifications requirements for these roles were expected to change over time as the new international locations reach operating status.) As a result, only minor wording changes were made to the qualifications provided by the HR department, with the expectation that the description of qualifications for the international roles will be revised in the future as specific new requirements are established.

Job qualifications requirements (also called minimum qualifications) are commonly used in making personnel selection and promotion decisions. Assessments and qualifications requirements used in making personnel decisions must adhere to professional and legal guidelines governing their development and validation. These guidelines include the *Uniform Guidelines on Employee Selection Procedures.*[4] There is a substantial body of literature on the identification and validation of job qualifications, and qualifications requirements have been the subject of a number of court cases and consent decrees.[5,6] Many large and medium-size organizations have established qualifications requirements for their jobs. These requirements often can be found in position descriptions. Confer with your organization's HR department regarding required qualifications. While including established qualifications requirements as part of a career path can be very useful, we generally recommend not establishing qualifications requirements as part of a career path project.

Information regarding occupation-specific licensure requirements in each state in the United States, and information about occupation-specific certifications, is available on the U.S. Department of Labor-sponsored CareerOneStop website (http://www.careeronestop.org). Information about training and education requirements for hundreds of occupations is provided in the *Occupational Outlook Handbook.*[7]

To identify recommended qualifications, it is generally useful to present any established required qualifications for the target jobs or occupations during career path workshops, and then ask questions such as those shown in the box below.

Questions to Solicit Information about Recommended Qualifications

- Review the required qualifications at level x. What additional education or training (if any) would you recommend that a person have to perform well at this level?
- What general types of experience would you recommend that a person have to perform well at this level?
- Are there certifications for this job that are not required, but that you would recommend obtaining?

Critical Developmental Experiences

Critical developmental experiences (CDEs) are experiences that a person at a specific point in his or her career should obtain to prepare for movement to the next career step. They include, for example, development programs, shadowing assignments, specific stretch assignments, leadership roles, and brief rotational assignments (lengthy rotational assignments are often portrayed as separate nodes on a career path). The sample Career Path Guide shown in Chapter 1 includes examples of critical developmental experiences for EPC, Inc. EPC, Inc. included CDEs that employees should target at a

---

Examples:
Critical Developmental Experiences

Example 1: Compile, analyze, and track data and statistical information

About this Experience:

- This experience involves compiling and managing data and deriving basic statistical information (such as percentages, changes in numbers over time, means and standard deviations), using spreadsheets in order to provide professional and efficient support in the employee's technical area.
- This experience should be gained at the x level on the career path.

Example 2: Contribute to policy development within employee's technical area

About this Experience:

- This experience entails identifying the need for revised or new policy, gathering information on relevant issues, and preparing pertinent policy documents. This experience provides insight into the steps involved in developing and changing policy.
- This experience should be gained at the x level on the career path.

Example 3: Manage the implementation of a program

About this Experience:

- This experience entails managing the implementation of a national or global program in the employee's specialty area. While the scope of the program may vary, it should include responsibility for the full range of implementation issues, including communications, scheduling, roll-out strategy, budget, and evaluation.
- This experience should be gained as a second line supervisor.

specific level to enhance their preparedness and potential for success at the next level. Some CDEs are generally recommended while others represent required experience (essentially a qualification) for the next level. Additional examples of critical developmental experiences are provided in the box on page 55.

In most cases, information about critical developmental experiences is obtained in interviews and workshops. In the EPC, Inc. case, information regarding these experiences was obtained during the career path workshops. Unlike most of the other career path components, an initial draft is typically not prepared prior to these sessions, because there are usually not available sources for this information other than the job experts participating in the interviews and workshops. However, a few examples should be provided to participants. Questions that can be used to solicit information about critical developmental experiences are shown in the box below.

Questions to Solicit Information about Critical Developmental Experiences

- What are the key developmental experiences that a person should obtain at this point in his or her career that will prepare him or her for the next career step?
- Are there specific stretch assignments that a person should seek at this point in his or her career?
- Are there important informal leadership roles (such as leading a team conducting a project) that a person should obtain at this point in his or her career to prepare him or her for more formal leadership roles?
- In thinking about your own experience and that of your colleagues, what were the experiences at step x in your career that made you ready to move to the next career step?

Competencies that are Accrued, Strengthened, or Required

Competencies can be defined as sets of knowledge, skills, and/or abilities that are applied to perform a task or a job. Career paths typically include information about the competencies that are accrued, strengthened, or required at each node on the path, or that are accrued or strengthened through each critical developmental experience. As noted previously, if the career paths are being designed primarily for workforce development purposes the competency information that is included will typically be more detailed than if the career paths are being designed for other purposes. In this case, descriptions of a large number of competencies (e.g., all competencies important for any relevant position) may be included in the career path document/web resource or associated documents. Including comprehensive lists of important competencies can be particularly useful if the career paths will link directly to a training and development curriculum. In most other cases, however, the number of competencies that are associated with any one point on a career path should be kept to a minimum. In general, the goal is not to be fully inclusive – it is to focus attention on what is most important.

In the EPC, Inc. case, a decision was made to include only a few competencies at each level that are most important to develop across all positions at that level. As noted in the Career Path Guide shown in Chapter 1, the EPC, Inc. Individual Development Planning Guide contains comprehensive lists of important competencies for each position, and employees at EPC, Inc. are encouraged to use that guide in conjunction with the Career Path Guide to identify specific development needs and priorities.

Competencies vary widely in level of specificity and complexity, from broad and basic (e.g., communication skills, professionalism) to specific and complex (e.g., Visual Basic programming skill, skill in performing cardiac catheterization). In some cases, information about the level of the competency (e.g., basic understanding, expert) that is required is included as part of a career path, while in other cases (such as the EPC, Inc. case) only a list of competencies and a brief definition of each is included. The appropriate level of detail of the competency information depends on the purposes for which the paths will be used. Examples of competencies with brief definitions are provided in the sample EPC, Inc. Career Path Guide (see Chapter 1). Additional examples are provided in the box on page 58.

Surveys As noted previously, initial information about competencies is often gathered using surveys. Surveys can be used to identify the competencies needed to perform a job, and the level of each of those competencies that is needed at each job level. Designing a competency survey that produces accurate information is both an art and

---

Examples:

Competencies

Basic Computer Operations – demonstrating a working knowledge of computer hardware and software, including operating and navigating through basic computer software, such as word processing programs and presentation software.

Recruiting/Staffing – the ability to apply knowledge of processes and procedures relating to advertising positions; candidate recruiting; and the testing/assessment, interviewing, processing, and hiring of candidates for positions.

Multimedia Technologies – skill in the application of principles, tools, and techniques for developing multimedia products using text, audio, and graphics.

---

a science. While instruction in the design of surveys to gather competency information is beyond the scope of this book, there have been thousands of articles and books published on survey design. In addition, many consulting firms and web-based survey vendors provide competency survey design and administration services.

Existing sources of information It can be very informative to conduct a survey to gather competency information for a career path project and doing so is sometimes the best option, particularly when the resulting information will be used for a variety of purposes. However, conducting a survey does take time and expertise. In lieu of a competency survey conducted specifically for a career path project, existing information can often be used to derive draft lists of competencies. These lists can then be refined to fit the specific requirements of the career path effort during workshops or interviews. This existing information may come from a variety of available sources. Three very useful sources are an organization's existing job analysis information, O*NET, and the U.S. Department of Labor's Competency Clearinghouse.

Job analysis is the foundation for a variety of human resources processes and systems and is conducted by many organizations. Job analysis is a systematic process used to gather detailed information about jobs. There are many methods for gathering job analysis information.[8] Oftentimes, job analysis information is gathered from job experts (typically job incumbents and first-line supervisors) via interviews, focus groups, and surveys. In most cases, information about tasks performed on jobs and the competencies required to perform those tasks is gathered as part of a job analysis. Competency information gathered as part of a job analysis can be very useful in developing career paths.

The U.S. Department of Labor's O*NET system provides a great deal of information about the competencies needed in most occupations. O*NET includes information on 277 variables, or "descriptors," for over 800 occupations.[9] These variables include knowledge areas, skills, abilities, work activities, interests, and work values. O*NET variables such as skills and abilities can be used in their original form in the competency component of career paths, or they can be combined into more general competencies.

The Competency Clearinghouse website (http://www.careeronestop.org/CompetencyModel/default.aspx), also sponsored by the U.S. Department of Labor, includes definitions of competencies that are important across most jobs, a tool for developing competency models (the sets of competencies needed for specific jobs or occupations), and links to existing competency models. This website can be very useful in deriving competency information for career paths.

Interviews and workshops If feasible, derive rough draft lists of key competencies that are accrued, strengthened, or required at each node in the initial draft career path prior to conducting formal interviews or workshops. If it is not feasible to do so, you should at least come up with a draft overall list of competencies associated with the target jobs before conducting the interviews or workshops. Explain to the participants what competencies are and how they will be used within the context of the career paths. Then, work with the participants to derive or refine competency information. Questions that can be used to gather information about the competencies that are accrued, strengthened, or required at various points on the career path are shown in the box on page 60. Choose specific questions based on the goals of your project and the nature of the information in the draft competency lists.

In the EPC, Inc. case, initial lists of competencies were derived based on information regarding important competencies in similar

Questions to Solicit Information about Competencies

- Review the draft list of competencies accrued or strengthened at the x level. Is this list accurate? Are any critical competencies that are developed at this career stage missing? Can any of the competencies on the list be deleted because they are not critical or not the focus of development at this career stage?
- Review the overall list of competencies associated with the job. Which, if any, of those competencies are accrued or strengthened at the first point in the career path? Are there additional competencies that are not on the overall list that should be included at this point in the path?
- What specific competencies would be strengthened through critical developmental experience x? What skills or capabilities does a person gain through that experience?
- Will job incumbents understand these competencies? If not, how should the competency names and/or definitions be edited?
- What level of this competency is required at this career stage (e.g., basic understanding, basic proficiency, expert level)?
- Does the relative importance of this competency increase or decrease at successive levels or roles in the organization? If so, how?
- Are there patterns or combinations of competencies that are valuable and should be identified in the path?

jobs in other organizations, and EPC, Inc. position descriptions and training materials. These competencies were reviewed by the POC and then included in a brief online survey completed by a representative sample of employees across the three functions at each relevant level (Individual Contributor, Leader, Senior Leader). Survey respondents indicated how important each competency was for successful performance of their jobs. The competencies the survey data showed to be most important were included in the materials presented in the workshops. Workshop participants added a few competencies based on anticipated job requirements in the future (particularly for the international roles), and made minor wording changes to several other competencies.

Career Success Factors

While it is desirable to address career success factors explicitly in career path documents/web resources, this information is frequently implicit in the career paths themselves. Regardless of whether you address these factors explicitly in career path documents/web resources (as EPC, Inc. did – see Chapter 1), it is very important to examine them when developing career paths. Doing so will result in richer career paths that more closely reflect the realities of your organization. It will allow you to explore and, in some cases, test "folk theories" regarding what leads to success in an organization. Finally, it can lead to an understanding of what is being reinforced (e.g., whether frequent movement among positions tends to lead to more promotions) and the extent to which there is alignment among the interests of individuals, business units, and the organization from a career path perspective (e.g., whether the frequency of movement that tends to lead to the greatest individual career success matches the frequency of movement that is best for the organization as a whole).

Career success factor questions were provided in Chapter 2. You should explore the success factor questions that are most relevant or salient to your organization. As a reminder, four career path attributes and one or two potential success factor questions relevant to each are shown in the box below.

Potential Career Success Factor Questions

- Movement. In general, what types of movement are most advantageous to a) individual success; b) organizational success? Can generalizations be made about the types of movement that are most advantageous, or does this depend completely on individual circumstances?
- Mobility. In general, how much movement is optimal for a) individual career success; b) organizational success?
- Expertise. Within a given career path, what is the relative value of breadth versus depth of expertise for a) individual career success; b) organizational success?
- Connectivity. To what extent are various career or occupational paths interconnected, and how might such connections be used for individual, organizational, or industry growth?

Analyses of human resources data can be used to explore what has – and has not – led to success in the past. Interviews and workshops can be used to identify perceptions of what leads to success, and to explore what organizational decision-makers feel is optimal for the organization given its strategy and direction.

Analyses of human resources data   Human resources databases can be used to examine what has occurred in the past and what has been associated with career success in the past. For example, HR data can be analyzed to determine how much movement there has been in the past within a given occupation, organizational unit, or organization, and the frequency and type of movement that tends to be associated with the greatest career success. Similarly, HR data can be used to test "folk theories" of what leads to success. For example, in one of our client companies, there was a common belief that promotion rates were greater in "line" organizations than in "support" organizations. This belief led some employees to gravitate to line organizations. However, analyses of human resources data revealed that promotion rates were actually higher in support organizations.

Interviews and workshops   As noted above, interviews and workshops can be used both to identify perceptions of what leads to success and to explore what organizational decision-makers feel is optimal for the organization given its strategy and direction. The opinions of organizational decision-makers regarding career success factors are particularly important when developing future-focused career paths. These decision-makers can impact promotion decisions and trends both by influencing organizational strategy that in turn influences hiring and promotion policies and numbers, and by having a voice in individual promotion decisions (particularly at the executive level).

Success factor questions such as those shown in the box "Potential Career Success Factor Questions" can be asked during the interviews and workshops. Carefully think through the questions you plan to ask prior to the workshops. Craft a set of questions that addresses the issues most important for the organization and/or occupation(s). However, don't stick too closely to a set of structured questions – use the prepared questions as a starting point for exploring important organizational issues, including whether there is a reasonable level of alignment between the interests of individuals, business units, and the organization. Executives tend to find these interviews valuable because they help them to think through important organizational issues that most executives rarely consider.

Remember that the answers to some questions (e.g., optimal frequency of movement, value of depth versus breadth) can differ widely within a given organization based on occupation and organizational unit. In addition, the answers to these questions can differ based on individual circumstances, the career aspirations of individual employees, etc. Acknowledge this variation at the beginning of the interview or focus group, and stress that you are seeking information about what tends to be the case given a specific career aspiration (e.g., reaching the highest technical level in the organization).

The Career Success Factors section of the EPC, Inc. Career Path Guide notes that three success factors were examined as part of the process of developing sales, marketing, and products career paths. These factors are breadth of knowledge and expertise, cross-geography experience, and optimal length of time in a position. These factors emerged as important areas to examine during discussions with the POC in the planning stages of the project. The first two factors (breadth of knowledge and expertise and cross-geography experience) were explored both in the initial interviews with executives and in the workshops with managers representing the three functions. The third factor (optimal length of time in a position) was examined both by analyzing HR data to determine the relationship between length of time in position and promotion rates, and by discussing this factor with executives and managers in the interviews and workshops.

Other Information

Other information about the roles or positions comprising a career path is sometimes provided as part of a description of career paths. This information will vary based on the purposes for which the career paths are being developed. It can include any information that you feel will be useful that is not included in the other components. Examples are salary information, anticipated growth rates in the occupation, and information about tasks or activities performed on the job. Salary information (including mean and median wages) and employment projections by occupation and industry are available on the U.S. Department of Labor's Bureau of Labor Statistics website (http://www.bls.gov/). (While this information can be very useful, company-specific salary information for the relevant jobs in your organization may be even more helpful to the target audience.) O*NET contains some information about activities and tasks performed in occupations.

Explicit Focus on Movement

As noted in Chapter 1, the potential and the promise of career paths lies in their focus on the movement of individuals among positions, assignments, jobs, and developmental experiences over a significant period of time. This movement represents the dynamic aspect of careers and talent management. It is the focus on movement that makes career paths valuable in career planning, succession management, and workforce planning. In our experience, most organizations and individuals do not spend adequate time thinking about movement from a system or career perspective. The focus tends to be on finding the next job, or on solving the staffing crisis of the day, rather than on systematic, long-term planning. In career path interviews and workshops, stress should be placed on providing information that will prepare people for movement. Thus, for example, when discussing competencies, the focus should be on the development of competencies that will maximize the person's preparedness for movement to other important positions in the organization.

Promoting Alignment

We noted earlier that career paths may stress the interests of the individual, organizational unit, organization, or industry. While this is true, career paths should promote the alignment of the interests of these entities, and should provide a linkage between individual career planning and organizational workforce planning. Ideally, the paths that are included will highlight opportunities that both maximize individual career potential and promote the organization's strategic vision. The EPC, Inc. career paths do just that.

Assessment of Personal Attributes and Career Paths

A thoughtful, long-term career perspective requires that people have some degree of self-insight into personal attributes that affect their choice of paths and their degree of career success. These include basic, stable individual attributes such as abilities, interests, values, and personality characteristics, and somewhat more malleable characteristics such as technical and interpersonal skills. In a career context, the subset of these characteristics (or the pattern of these characteristics) that can have a pivotal impact on success or failure can be labeled enablers and potential derailers. Enablers are key personal characteristics that facilitate a person's success in a specific work environment. Potential derailers are key personal characteristics that can result in failure in a specific work environment.

People have varying levels of awareness, and acceptance, of their personal attributes. While not explicitly part of a career path, understanding these characteristics is very important both in choosing the right path and in growth and development along that path.

Many tools and methodologies to assess career path attributes are available for use by individuals and organizations in career planning and development. These include, for example, measures of personality, interests, values, skills, and abilities. Most of these tools are now available online and thus can be administered and scored very efficiently. Assessment centers that include a variety of assessment exercises including role plays are used by many organizations to provide a comprehensive view of individuals' (typically managers') strengths and developmental needs. An in-depth discussion of individual career planning and the assessment of personal attributes is beyond the scope of this book. However, we would like to stress that when developing and implementing career paths and associated talent management systems, organizations should consider the role of assessment in career planning and development, acknowledge the importance of self-insight into one's attributes, and integrate assessment opportunities into career planning and development programs.

Implementation Tips

Many, perhaps most, human capital tools that are developed are never fully implemented. In some cases this is because they do not meet the needs of the organization. However, more often than not, it is for reasons unrelated to the quality of the tools or the extent to which they meet organizational needs. In this section we provide tips that will help to ensure that the career paths you construct are implemented and used.

First, it is very important to have high-level support for any human capital effort, including a career path effort. Having a champion at a high level in the organization helps to ensure the participation of job experts in the development phase, and also to ensure that the career paths are implemented and used by the organization.

Second, you should stress the practical benefits of the career paths to particular stakeholder groups from the beginning. Because career paths have benefits for multiple stakeholders (employees, managers, executives), you can shape your message to fit the audience by stressing the real benefits of career paths for a particular group.

Third, integrate the career paths with existing or new talent management tools and systems, such as training, career development, succession management, and strategic workforce planning tools and systems. We discuss how to do this in Chapters 4 and 5. For now, the important point is that the career paths will be used and will help your organization and its employees succeed if they are an integral component of your organization's talent management systems. They are unlikely to be used if they are developed and implemented in isolation of those systems.

Fourth, there are certain considerations that you should stress to job experts, managers, and employees during both the development and implementation phases that will help to ensure that the career paths are used properly and that they are seen as tools that genuinely help people to succeed rather than as constraints that limit success. These include:

- The career paths provide a great deal of valuable information about how to achieve success in an organization, occupation, or industry. However, the career paths are not the only paths to success. There are many possible paths to a successful and fulfilling career, some of which may be idiosyncratic to a single person.
- Individuals must be encouraged and supported to develop in their current jobs as much as in the pursuit of future roles or jobs. In most cases, neither the organization nor the individual will give the appropriate time to development in the pursuit of future roles or positions if there is not some benefit in the current job (e.g., improvement in performance on a performance dimension that is important in the person's current job).
- The career paths do not represent a "check the box" system. Even if a person obtains all of the critical developmental experiences, masters the competencies listed, etc., there is no guarantee that he or she will be promoted to a given level in the organization. There

are factors in addition to those addressed in the career paths that affect promotions, including factors over which the employee has no control – such as headcount restrictions at specific organizational levels. Similarly, employees can be promoted without doing everything that is recommended at a given level.

• Recommendations provided in career paths should be viewed as recommendations and not as requirements, unless they are explicitly stated as such.

The Bottom Line

The process of developing career paths is straightforward. In most cases, it involves gathering existing information about jobs and occupations, and then holding interviews and workshops with job experts using the procedures described in this chapter. While the approach is simple, much of the value of developing career paths lies in the fact that it can and should spur thinking about complex and fundamental issues regarding the movement of individuals through careers within and across organizations. These issues have immediate implications for a variety of important organizational systems and processes, such as workforce planning, succession management, and individual career development.

Chapter 4

Integrating Career Paths into Talent Management Systems I:
Recruitment, Hiring, Retention, Promotion, and Employee Development

As discussed in earlier chapters, integrating career paths into your organization's overall talent management system allows your organization to offer enhanced value propositions, manage employee movement and flow, and organize both short- and long-term talent development. As a result, career paths can improve the effectiveness of your organization's recruitment and hiring processes, retention and promotion strategies, and training and development programs.

In this chapter, we explore the application of career paths to recruitment, hiring, retention, promotion, and ongoing training and development. That is, we explore how career paths serve as practical tools and guiding resources in attracting, developing, and retaining talent, all critical elements in maintaining your organization's viability. Before addressing these topics, however, we discuss two factors that have significant implications for the use of career paths in support of all of the talent management system components discussed in this chapter and in Chapter 5 – how to "connect" the employee to the organization in today's world, and how to engage the new workforce.

Connecting the Employee to the Organization

Creating a "contract" between the organization and individuals/groups sounds "old school" but is actually more important than ever.

In this case, the contract we are referencing is not a legally-binding document of any kind. Rather, the contract is psychological, emotional, and motivational. This contract represents how strongly the employee is connected to the organization – on many levels.

Both academic and applied research indicates that employees have greater expectations than ever for what organizations should provide in exchange for their loyalty and tenure. In the late 1990s, Sullivan, Carden, and Martin presented an aggregate review of the career research literature that supported this observable shift in the relationship between employees and organizations.[1] The authors concluded that workers at all levels will increasingly follow non-linear career paths that are influenced primarily by two factors:

1. transferability and marketability of competencies and portable skills;
2. strength of the implied contract between the employee and the organization (labeled "internal work values" by the authors).

The authors propose a career grid based upon these two factors. Employees with more portable skills and a corresponding strong identification with their profession are less likely to feel connected to the organization and therefore are at greater risk to leave. For our purposes, their research and proposed typology provides logical support for the importance that organizations should place on "connecting" employees to the organization itself just as strongly as they used to endeavor to connect employees to specific jobs within the organization.

In addition to engendering implied or "psychological" contracts with employees, organizations should also establish explicit contracts with valuable talent. Such a contract can take the form of a development plan with a timeline, a special assignment with specific learning goals and outcomes to achieve, or the creation of a specialized "next role" in the organization. The contract should not take the form of an assumption that individuals know why they are valued, what opportunities they should pursue within the organization, or what doors might be open to them in the future. Career paths support the development and maintenance of such contracts by fostering clear and open communication with employees.

Career paths help to minimize incorrect assumptions by providing a clear, objective structure for managers and mentors to utilize when reviewing options and progress with their employees. They can pin-point where an employee is stagnating, missing an opportunity, or might be able to go next in the organization. This clarity is especially important with frontline, traditionally hourly jobs. Regarding such jobs, it is particularly important that organizations proactively communicate "where you can go" to employees. These employees often make job and employer choices based on small wage and benefit

---

Jessica Nicolo's Story

Jessica's rapid progress down the path

Jessica Nicolo joined EchoStar Communications Corp. as a phone-based customer service agent. In less than one year, she was promoted three times. She now has a role in which she supports other agents with challenging customer calls. Within two years, her wages at EchoStar have increased by 27%.

A welcome change

Jessica's previous call center jobs had been less satisfying. She was in her previous job at another company for less than one year. She sees her future at her current employer as full of possibilities, citing support from supervisors and open access to career progression opportunities at the company.

What's different at EchoStar?

The company implemented a career path program with the intent of increasing retention among their call center employees. They wanted to cut their hiring and training costs and create more opportunities for people to advance in the organization.

What's next?

Within two years, the average company tenure among call center agents has increased from nine months to nineteen months. Agents have access to skill development and training that enables them to advance both in the call center and beyond to other roles in the company.

Jessica has her eye on a position that she knows is several years away from her current role. But, she is motivated because the path to get there is clear and supported by her supervisors. She can also track her career progress using an in-house software system.

Source: Badal (2006)

increases. Organizations must help these employees to see their future as a career rather than a series of disconnected jobs.

Many larger organizations, such as Burger King and Bank of America, are now reaching down to the frontlines in their organizations to identify future talent.[2] These organizations have developed concrete programs to share opportunities for advancement with employees from the moment they are hired. Consider the example in the box on page 71, adapted from a story in *The Wall Street Journal Online*.[3]

The approach taken by EchoStar is an excellent example of how organizations can leverage career paths to establish a new type of contract with their employees. Jessica knows that opportunities for more meaningful work and more money are ahead for her at the company. Since the career path to continue her progress is known and public, she can plan and track her movement along the path. In return for such opportunities, Jessica fulfills her side of the contract with strong performance, loyalty, and tenure – eliminating the company's costs to recruit, hire, and train and develop her replacement. Multiply Jessica's story by dozens, possibly even hundreds, of employees at her organization and you get a sense of the cost savings and other talent retention benefits for the organization.

Engaging the New Workforce

Following popular trends, today's workers, especially newer graduates, have been characterized as a type of "What's in it for me (WIFM)?" generation. This generation is often collectively referred to as Generation Y, or simply Gen Y. Gen Y refers to the 70 million Americans born between 1978 and 2002 that are entering the U.S. workforce at a rapid pace, comprising more than 20% of the workforce.[4]

Another characterization of this group is that even committed Gen Y workers, without intended shortsightedness or egocentricity, are developing with a perspective that organizations have the responsibility to "keep me here." However, little solid research evidence is available to test such claims. One study, conducted across several Finnish organizations, did identify meaningful differences between employees under the age of thirty-five and those over the age of fifty.[5]

The study found that older workers generally expect the organization to support success in their current job, and they expect to be provided with a meaningful job. In contrast, the younger employees emphasized the need for career opportunities and challenging jobs. Older employees also tended to feel that the value of developing at the organization was in helping them to "stay at work" and to achieve outcomes for the organization. The younger employees emphasized development that supports career progress and enables them to update their work skills. Of note, such differences between older and younger cohorts may be present regardless of the particular time-frame or set of generations of interest.

As such, engaging younger workers with opportunities for clear, achievable "wins" in as short as three to six months (and typically no more than two years) is important as part of the organization's longer-term strategy. Youthful competitiveness can fuel a strong work ethic as well as impatience to be recognized and rewarded as a valuable part of the workforce.[6]

Career paths can help organizations engage younger generations by showing them how they can achieve "wins" and by providing concrete information about the career opportunities available to them. You should start with an analysis of your current workforce – age, skills, roles, hiring patterns, etc. Then create a picture of where the organization is headed. Develop, refine, and communicate career paths within that context. Will you increasingly hire younger workers? If so, you should expect to face unique developmental challenges.

While you will hear a wealth of anecdotal wisdom about generational differences, it is very important to keep in mind that all employees within a generational cohort (e.g., Gen Y) are not the same. Treating them as the same can amount to stereotypical thinking. Generally, owing to individual differences, there is more variance within generational groups than between. Thus, development and career path programs should be tailored to fit the real needs of individual employees and should not be based on broad characterizations of generational groups that may or may not be accurate.

Recruitment and Hiring

Career paths can be used to increase your organization's competitive advantage in the recruiting and hiring arenas in several ways. First, career paths can help you to sell potential employees on a career rather than an entry-level job. Most potential new hires, particularly in knowledge worker roles, aspire to move beyond the role for which they are applying. Clearly articulating the growth opportunities and potential movement subsequent to the initial role can often increase recruits' overall attraction to the role and the organization. This can be particularly effective for organizations recruiting for higher-volume, entry-level positions. Retention problems are often associated with these positions because they typically offer relatively low pay, and competitors often can steal employees with just a small wage increase. Helping new hires, and incumbents, to understand the future opportunities that might be available in the organization can lead to increased hiring success and improved retention.

Many companies use career paths as a recruiting tool. The Internet provides a particularly effective means for presenting career paths in a consistent, visually engaging manner. Figure 4.1 provides an excellent example from Whole Foods Market. Whole Foods was rated number 16 in Fortune's 100 Best Companies to Work For in 2008.[7] The information shown in Figure 4.1 (excerpted from their career website) clearly and simply communicates the company's perspective toward career path management and provides potential job seekers with an understanding of the career paths in the Stores, Facilities, Regional Offices, and Global Headquarters sectors of the organization.

This career site content shows clearly how Whole Foods Market is using career paths to communicate both the breadth and depth of opportunities available in the company. Job seekers can see the range of areas in which opportunities are available. More importantly, several career paths are offered, showing the progression from entry-level roles to senior leadership roles.

Second, sharing information about career paths and potential opportunities for advancement as early as the recruiting stage can result in increased employee loyalty among those who are hired. Employees recognize which organizations place more emphasis on growth and advancement. Employees who enter the organization understanding the potential for a long-term, fulfilling career in the organization are much more likely to enter with the intent of staying over an extended period and are thus more likely to feel some sense of loyalty and commitment to the organization from day one.[8]

Figure 4.1 Career Path Information from Whole Foods Market, Inc.

Source: http://www.wholefoodsmarket.com/careers/paths.html.

Career Paths

Whole Foods Market seeks individuals who believe in our mission of Whole Foods, Whole People, Whole Planet – people who are enthusiastic about food and our products, and who want to join a culture of shared fate.

We mentor our team members through education and on-the-job experience. We encourage participation and involvement at all levels of our business. Team expertise is developed by fostering creativity, self-responsibility and self-directed teamwork, and by rewarding productivity and performance.

Opportunities That Grow With You

We encourage all qualified team members to apply for any available opportunity in their store or facility, their region or the company as they expand their product knowledge, develop their skills and enhance their value to their teams. To support advancement from within, all openings for positions at team leader level and higher are listed on our internal job site. Many other openings are posted as well, from all around the company.

Opportunities in Our Stores

Departments	
- Bakery	Store Team Leaders
- Customer Service	Associate Store Team Leaders
- Grocery	
- Facilities	Specialized Store Support*
- Floral	Department Team Leaders
- Meat	
- Prepared Foods	Associate Team Leaders
- Produce	
- Seafood	Specialized Team Members**
- Specialty	
- Whole Body	Team Members

Department Descriptions   * HB, Accounting, IT/Store Systems, Marketing
                           ** Buyers, Specialists, Receivers, Supervisors,
                              Chefs/Cooks, Estheticians, etc.

Opportunities in Our Facilities

Facility Types	
- Bakehouses	Facility Team Leaders
- Coffee-Roasting Operation	Associate Facility Team Leaders
- Commissary Kitchens	Buyers
- Distribution Warehouses	Team Leaders
- Seafood Processing & Distribution	Associate Team Leaders/Supervisors
	Team Members

continued

Opportunities in Our Regional Offices

Areas

- Accounting
- Administration
- Construction
- HR
- IT & Store Systems
- Marketing
- Product Area Leadership

Regional Presidents

Regional Vice Presidents

Senior Coordinators

Coordinators/Associate Coordinators

Product Buyers and Merchandisers

Team Leaders

Specialized Team Members

Opportunities at Our Global Headquarters

Areas

- Accounting/Finance
- Administration
- HR
- Investor Relations
- IT
- Legal
- Marketing
- Procurement & Distribution
- Real Estate/ Construction

Presidents

Executive Vice Presidents

Global Vice Presidents

Senior Coordinators

Group Leaders

Team Leaders

Specialized Team Members

Department Descriptions

- Bakery: production and customer service; may include coffee and/or juice bar
- Customer Service: cash registers and customer service booth
- Facilities: store maintenance and janitorial staff
- Floral: cut flowers, bouquets and plants; may include gardening supplies, gift baskets
- Grocery: grocery, frozen foods, dry goods, dairy and bulk foods
- Meat: fresh, frozen and smoked natural meats and poultry
- Prepared Foods: production and customer service; may include "restaurant" venues, juice bar
- Produce: fresh and packaged produce items; may include cut fruit and vegetables, fresh juices
- Seafood: fresh, frozen and smoked seafood
- Specialty: cheese, wine and beer; may include coffee, housewares, chocolate and charcuterie
- Whole Body: nutritional supplements, body care and books/cards/magazines; may include gifts, housewares, natural lifestyle products (organic clothing and linens, etc.)

In a recruiting context, emphasis should be placed on the visual depiction of the steps along the career paths. The idea is to capture the imagination of recruits, and help them to see that your organization offers fulfilling, long-term career potential. Such clear, visual representations can be a boon to recruiting in part because they provide immediate answers to many potential applicant questions. In the context of Whole Foods Market, these questions may include the following examples. "If I join the Stores segment of the organization, where might I go in the future?" "I want to be a buyer; how can I get there at Whole Foods Market?" "What should I expect to do before I am ready to become a leader in this organization?" Clear career path diagrams and concise supporting information can address such questions.

Third, developing career paths can help you and your hiring managers more clearly understand qualification and competency requirements for jobs at all levels across the career path. This understanding, coupled with a carefully developed selection process that is demonstrated to be job-relevant, can help you to improve the hiring process, resulting in hires who not only have the qualifications to perform an entry-level job, but who also have the potential to move into other roles over time, given appropriate development opportunities. Thus, for hiring purposes, you should attend to the qualifications and competency information in your organization's career paths.

As discussed in Chapter 3, it is very useful to include established qualifications requirements as part of a career path. However, we generally recommend not establishing qualifications requirements as part of a career path project because there are specific guidelines and standards that must be followed to demonstrate that qualifications requirements are job-relevant. We also strongly recommend that you confer with your organization's HR and legal departments when you are considering how to use career path information in a hiring context.

The advantages career paths can provide in recruiting and hiring don't end with the hiring decision. Career paths can also be a very useful tool to help employees become acclimated to your organization in the early phases of employment – often referred to as "on-boarding." When individuals are on-boarded to the organization, they begin the process of learning their job/role requirements, company structure and policies, and the company culture – both formal and informal.

Many organizations include initial performance planning and/or development planning at this point in the employee lifecycle. Employees will typically have performance targets for a set timeframe (e.g., six or twelve months) and a means to measure their performance at regular intervals. A similar approach can be taken for development planning. New employees can identify goals for learning, "stretching" their performance, and otherwise increasing their knowledge and skills. Success in these endeavors increases their value to the organiza-

Figure 4.2 Career Path Information from Quicken Loans, Inc.
Source: http://www.quickenloanscareers.com/web/teams/mortgage/Roadmap.pdf; used with permission

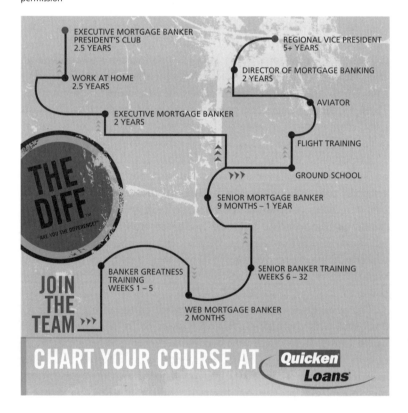

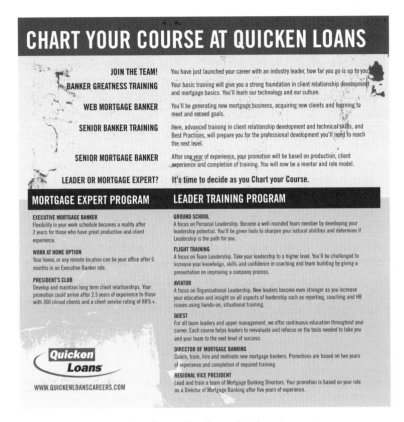

CHART YOUR COURSE AT QUICKEN LOANS

JOIN THE TEAM! You have just launched your career with an industry leader, how far you go is up to you!

BANKER GREATNESS TRAINING Your basic training will give you a strong foundation in client relationship development and mortgage basics. You'll learn our technology and our culture.

WEB MORTGAGE BANKER You'll be generating new mortgage business, acquiring new clients and learning to meet and exceed goals.

SENIOR BANKER TRAINING Here, advanced training in client relationship development and technical skills, and Best Practices, will prepare you for the professional development you'll need to reach the next level.

SENIOR MORTGAGE BANKER After one year of experience, your promotion will be based on production, client experience and completion of training. You will now be a mentor and role model.

LEADER OR MORTGAGE EXPERT? It's time to decide as you Chart your Course.

MORTGAGE EXPERT PROGRAM

EXECUTIVE MORTGAGE BANKER
Flexibility in your work schedule becomes a reality after 2 years for those who have great production and client experience.

WORK AT HOME OPTION
Your home, or any remote location can be your office after 6 months in an Executive Banker role.

PRESIDENT'S CLUB
Develop and maintain long term client relationships. Your promotion could arrive after 2.5 years of experience to those with 300 closed clients and a client service rating of 88%+.

LEADER TRAINING PROGRAM

GROUND SCHOOL
A focus on Personal Leadership. Become a well-rounded team member by developing your leadership potential. You'll be given tools to sharpen your natural abilities and determine if Leadership is the path for you.

FLIGHT TRAINING
A focus on Team Leadership. Take your leadership to a higher level. You'll be challenged to increase your knowledge, skills and confidence in coaching and team building by giving a presentation on improving a company process.

AVIATOR
A focus on Organizational Leadership. New leaders become even stronger as you increase your education and insight on all aspects of leadership such as reporting, coaching and HR issues using hands-on, situational training.

QUEST
For all team leaders and upper management, we offer continuous education throughout your career. Each course helps leaders to reevaluate and refocus on the tools needed to take you and your team to the next level of success.

DIRECTOR OF MORTGAGE BANKING
Coach, train, hire and motivate new mortgage bankers. Promotions are based on two years of experience and completion of required training.

REGIONAL VICE PRESIDENT
Lead and train a team of Mortgage Banking Directors. Your promotion is based on your role as a Director of Mortgage Banking after five years of experience.

Quicken Loans

WWW.QUICKENLOANSCAREERS.COM

Figure 4.2 Career Path Information from Quicken Loans, Inc.

tion. This type of early planning can benefit from career paths. Managers and new employees can use career path information to identify specific, relevant focus areas to target for growth and development. Using career path information for such planning can accelerate employee growth and increase your organization's internal talent pool for future openings. Consider the career path information from Quicken Loans (rated number two on the Fortune 100 Best Companies to Work For in 2008[9]) in Figure 4.2.

Quicken Loans uses career paths as an engaging communication device to convey how positions are connected and the typical minimum time requirement for each position. The path summary also provides a concise overview of both leader training and flexible employment options (e.g., work at home) for job seekers to consider. The information available on the Quicken Loans site provides a very specific picture of what a new hire can expect in the form of time in role, time in training, and the specific sequence of roles and development activities. A job seeker can see very clearly how he or she will spend time in the first year on the job at Quicken Loans. This specific information helps employees establish realistic expectations. Additionally, the path to a Regional Vice President or Executive Mortgage Banker is also available for consideration. This type of information can be a powerful motivator for ambitious employees.

In summary, career paths can help organizations in the recruitment, hiring, and on-boarding processes by allowing them to sell applicants on a career rather than an entry-level job, by demonstrating the commitment of the organization to continued career growth, by clearly identifying the qualifications and competency requirements for jobs, and by helping to establish realistic expectations for career growth among new employees.

Retention

Career paths, when integrated into your organization's overall talent management strategy, can help your organization to retain valued employees in several ways. First, they promote a sense of fairness and consistency in how the company makes decisions. Second, as noted in the previous section, they promote a sense of loyalty and commitment among employees by demonstrating the commitment of the organization to long-term career development and by clearly showing the potential for a long-term, fulfilling career in the organization. Third, they take the guesswork out of career progression and development for employees. By doing so, career paths help employees to see how they can achieve their career goals without leaving the organization and, importantly, they give employees a sense that they have some degree of control over their futures.

All five of the career path components shown in the box "Fundamental Components of Career Paths" in Chapter 1 are relevant to retention. A sequential list of positions or roles helps employees to understand their career options and the career potential offered by the organization. Listing qualifications requirements, competencies, and critical developmental experiences demonstrates some degree of objectivity and fairness in company decisions, and helps employees see how they need to develop over the short and long term to achieve their career goals. Finally, information about career success factors helps employees to understand the types and nature of movement that will help them most in their careers with the organization, and thus provides employees with a sense that career progression within the organization is not based completely on factors beyond their control, and that they have some control over their career trajectories.

Proactively retaining employees requires clearly defined performance requirements (so people know what is expected of them), clear paths for movement (so people understand their future options), and clear criteria for promotions (so people feel that there is a transparent and level playing field).

Look back to the case example in Chapter 1. You can see clearly how paths such as those constructed for EPC, Inc. can impact retention. You are given a very clear picture of what is required or relevant to move from one role to another. Clarity of this kind goes a long way in creating perceptions of fairness and consistency in how the company makes decisions. When requirements are ambiguous or vary according to who is relating them to an employee, questions arise about the true criteria for getting ahead. Another benefit of being clear about requirements is that doing so gives employees the information they need to identify paths or roles that they do not want to pursue. They are then equipped to select another path or to possibly leave the organization altogether (some turnover can be healthy for all concerned).

Promotion

Career paths can improve the quality of promotion decisions by showing, in a clear and simple manner, the requirements, characteristics, and experiences that are important for various jobs, roles, or levels in an organization. This information can be useful to managers when they are comparing employee qualifications and experiences to requirements for positions in the context of a promotion decision. This information can also be useful when providing information about why an employee was or was not promoted, and what the employee can do to improve his or her chances of being promoted in the future. (As with hiring, we recommend that you confer with your organization's HR and legal departments when you are considering how to use career path information in a promotion context.)

Managers consider several inputs when determining the viability of a candidate for promotion. Example inputs typically include current and past performance data, tenure with the organization, and known experiences and knowledge gained in the organization. Other inputs can include assessment results and one's reputation in the organization. In total, promotion decisions are always a balance of two critical components – demonstrated past performance and future potential. The profile of the individual (both with regard to past performance and future potential) can be compared to both the requirements of the target job/role and to the anticipated needs and direction of the organization.

As noted above, career path information can be used to guide promotion decisions by showing the requirements, characteristics, and experiences that are important for various jobs, roles, or levels in an organization. Thus, the qualifications, competencies, and critical developmental experiences components of career paths are most relevant to promotion decisions. This information can be used when considering the potential of employees for specific roles in the immediate future, and the long-term potential of employees for more distal roles. Consider the story of Jill Evans presented in Figure 4.3 (see page 84).

Jill's story is obviously more the exception rather than the norm. Yet, the story is an example of how organizations should view their talent in the context of both current and future needs. Jill didn't know exactly where her career was headed in her company. However, she had examined the company's career path documents and had taken them to heart. While her specific career path was not laid out in these documents, she was able to use these documents to gain an understanding of the competencies and experiences she needed to accrue to succeed in the organization, and of how the company's strategy was relevant to her career growth and development. She also knew she was enjoying her work, doing it well, and being offered exciting new roles and experiences along the way. The company recognized her talent, moved her where they needed such talent, supported her ongoing growth in a systematic fashion (as articulated in the company's career path documents and related developmental resources), and positioned her to be successful if she continued to perform well. When the urgent need for a senior player arose unexpectedly, the senior team was able to promote one of their own because they had groomed a talented individual who was now both broad and deep. Using information from the career path documents, the senior team was able to clearly communicate to the rest of the organization exactly why Jill was the right choice.

An unfortunate outcome of many promotion decisions is that one or more highly qualified individuals are not selected for the new opportunity. Career paths can help the organization in this regard as well. Individuals not selected for an internal opening often have some level of reaction of "why not me?" Employees often, and quite reasonably, argue that they meet the stated requirements of the open job or role. If the organization is not careful in responding to these employees, they risk de-motivating or even losing those employees.

Properly positioned, career paths can serve as a motivator and guide to those not chosen for an opening. The path information provides a means for the manager to communicate objectively the why of the decision. The employee in turn can identify additional opportunities for growth to enhance his or her readiness for a future role.

Development Planning and Execution

In cases in which career paths are designed primarily for training and development purposes, comprehensive lists of important competencies required in each job, role, or level represented in the career paths, and lists of available training and development opportunities relevant to each of those competencies, are sometimes developed. (In this type of effort, the amount of information can be overwhelming if provided in a document, so a web-based development resource is usually designed with links that allow easy access to the specific information relevant to individual managers and employees.) In addition, information about gaps in available training and development resources (i.e., important competencies for which adequate training and development opportunities are not currently available) may be gathered as part of the project. Thus, projects in which career paths are designed primarily for training and development purposes are often combined career path development and training needs assessment efforts.

A promising young talent emerges

1

Entry level Consultant U.S. - Corporate 2½ years

Jill was hired 10 years ago as a young consultant in a successful, growth-oriented product and services organization. Jill began in a client implementation role and quickly learned all of the company's offerings. She was seen as a solid project manager and the field sales team sought her out for technical sales support. As the company grew, Jill expressed her interest in their international operations. After 2½ years with the company, Jill made her first significant move.

Off to Europe...

2

Senior Consultant Europe 1½ years

Jill was offered a position in Europe, living in London. She remained an individual contributor but established herself as an informal leader in project design, client implementation and strategic sales. She quickly expanded her knowledge of the company's global business and competitive landscape. The company continued to grow around the world, particularly in the emerging Asia/Pacific markets. After 18 months in Europe, Jill made her second significant move.

G'day mate!

3

Consulting Manager Australia 15 months

The company needed someone with Jill's talent to support their strategic growth in the Asia/Pacific region. Jill spoke only English so they agreed she would be best suited for Australia. She moved to Sydney and assumed her first formal leadership role in the company. Jill managed the consulting teams in Sydney and Melbourne. During her 15 months in Australia, she not only increased the local expertise and market share but also increased the connection between Australia and Asia, particularly Singapore. It was just after her 5 year anniversary with the company that Jill agreed to make her third significant move.

Figure 4.3 Jill's Story

The right move?

4

Consulting Manager/Strategic Account Manager U.S.-Midwest 2 years

Jill was asked to return to the U.S. to assume a role that looked to be much less glamorous than her recent international experiences. She assumed a mixed role in the Midwest office of the company. She led a sizable consulting team for 75% of her time and spent the remaining 25% in a strategic accounts role with a significant revenue goal. This mixed role provided Jill with a unique opportunity to truly understand the relationship between the sales/business development (accountable for revenue) and client consulting/implementation (accountable for costs and profit) arms of the organization. Again, Jill was very successful in her role and she increasingly thrived for 2 years until her final significant move.

It all pays off for Jill

5

Senior Vice President U.S. Corporate 4 years (and counting)

The company released a poor performing Senior Vice President who had been running one of the three primary product/service line. This line of business was responsible for nearly 30% of their global revenue. To the surprise of some, Jill was identified as a candidate for the opening. This role was 2–3 levels above her current role and no one on the senior team was as young in age or had as little tenure as Jill. After an internal assessment process with a handful of qualified candidates, Jill was promoted into the Senior VP role.

How did it all come together?

Jill was seen as qualified for the significant opening largely due to the portfolio of competencies and experiences she had gained in her career journey. Her blend of domestic and international experience, consulting and sales successful track record, and leadership of both individuals and teams formed the foundational elements of the success profile for the more senior role. Although she had never held a role in the corporate business unit she now leads, she sold, designed, implemented, and educated others in the organization about their offerings. Jill remains in her senior role. Under her leadership, the business unit has grown by double digits for the last three years, with record revenues and significant global expansion.

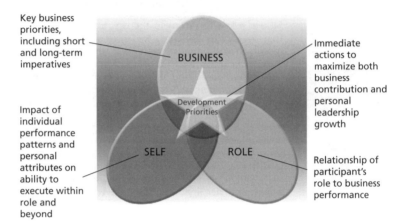

Key business priorities, including short and long-term imperatives

Impact of individual performance patterns and personal attributes on ability to execute within role and beyond

BUSINESS

Development Priorities

SELF   ROLE

Immediate actions to maximize both business contribution and personal leadership growth

Relationship of participant's role to business performance

Figure 4.4 Business/Role/Self Model
Source: Development Dimensions International; used with permission.

In a recent project of this nature conducted by one of the authors of this book, the end product (which contained comprehensive information about a variety of different potential career paths, the competencies required at each step along each of those, and the available training and development opportunities associated with each competency) was originally labeled a career roadmap. However, the client renamed it a career atlas, noting that, like a road atlas, it gave employees and their managers the information they needed to chart a detailed course with many different potential end-points and many potential developmental routes for reaching those end-points.

Figure 4.4 presents a model that is useful for guiding development choices and planning. It suggests a joint focus upon the perspectives of the Business, Role, and Self in planning careers and career paths.

The emphasis in this model is on identifying the "sweet spot" that maximizes benefits to the business, role, and the individual. Specifically, development provides maximum impact when it targets the motivations and aspirations of the individual employee, fulfills the requirements of the role, and directly supports the broader business. To the extent that any of the three "customers" of development are not considered, then development, and its value to the organization, is sub-optimized.

Progress along a career path can be accelerated with a development focus on Business/Role/Self (B/R/S). A variety of individual development plans and/or "career worksheets" can be constructed to explore the intersections of B/R/S. Let's return for a minute to the EPC organization from Chapter 1. Suppose a Sales Coordinator, we'll call him Joe, has progressed through a Sales Representative role and is now a Product Manager. Joe's true passion is sales and he aspires to become a Sales and Marketing Manager. He's been coached to look at his experiences, strengths, and development needs in light of the management role. He is also trying to consider how his current job is changing as the company business grows rapidly and shifts in focus. Joe and his supervisor have worked together to draft the worksheet in the box "Career Path Worksheet for Aspiring Sales and Marketing Manager" (page 88–89) to help him craft a focused development plan based on information in EPC Inc.'s Career Path Guide. The box provides a snapshot of Joe's career relative to the requirements along the path. Joe and his supervisor have captured several key factors that will drive Joe's continued movement along the career path. Joe identified these factors by asking questions focused on the Business/Role/Self intersection such as:

- Self: What am I motivated to do next?
- Role: What is the current and anticipated value of my role in the organization?
- Business: What are the short- and long-term organizational priorities that I can impact?

Joe emerges from his analysis with a strong sense of where he is and where he wants to go in the organization. Through a good deal of questioning, he also has a clear idea of how his role is shifting and what the expectations for his performance will be in the next year. Finally, he is confident that he understands the vision for the company's future and how changes are occurring to ensure competitive differentiation and growth. Joe now has to document his development plan, share it with his manager, and make it happen!

Once the development planning process has been completed, ensuring successful development execution becomes the focus. Although the employee should have primary accountability for success, the manager and the broader organization should provide the guidance and tools needed to maximize the chances of success. In addition to removing obstacles and barriers to successful execution, the organization can also provide a means for evaluating and communicating development progress. Practical experience tells us that development progress is much greater when employee develop-

Career Path Worksheet for Aspiring Sales and Marketing Manager		
Career Path Component	**Current Status** What has Joe done along the path to date?	**Action Planning** What are key B/R/S considerations for Joe's next steps?
Positions or Roles held	• Sales Coordinator • Sales Representative • Product Manager	• Motivated to continue growth toward a sales executive role • Product Manager role opportunities will increase with international expansion
Qualifications	✓ Education requirements met ✓ Cross-function experience obtained	• Strong relevant skills base, particularly in sales • Above average depth for current tenure but slightly narrow relative to others in role • Breadth key at all levels of organization to support growth on multiple fronts
Development Experiences	✓ Basic financial acumen training completed ✓ Sales foundation series completed ✓ Has cross-function experience ✗ Lacking cross-geography experience	• Motivated to continue to expand breadth beyond direct sales area • Lack of cross-geography experience is a hole

Career Path Component	Current Status What has Joe done along the path to date?	Action Planning What are key B/R/S considerations for Joe's next steps?
Competencies	✓ Focus on Customer ✓ Positive Working Relationships ✓ Business Acumen ✓ Market Focus ✗ Influencing Others ✗ Results Focus ✗ Leadership competencies in general	• Recognizes need to develop leadership competencies • Very unlikely to progress to next level of management without additional leadership experience • International business growth and retirements ensure new leadership opportunities
Career Success Factors/Facets	Organization places most value on: • agile players vs. experts • breadth vs. depth of knowledge and experience • experiential learning vs. extensive formal training	• Must balance passion for Sales with broader value points of the company • Competency weaknesses must be addressed • Likely to be 12–18 months away from being viable candidate for next level role

ment plans are documented in a measurable way and the manager is involved in development planning and evaluation.

Development progress discussions should include a discussion of career path implications for development progress. Managers should directly connect relevant development progress to one or more career paths so that employees can understand their progress not only in their current role but also against success requirements for future potential roles.

The Bottom Line

The quality of your organization's talent, and the ability of your organization to retain that talent, is without a doubt one of the most critical factors driving the success of your organization. Career paths, when integrated into your organization's talent management system, can play an important role in ensuring that your organization is able to attract and retain talented employees, and develop the skills of those employees in a manner that is aligned with current and future organizational needs.

Chapter 5

Integrating Career Paths into Talent Management Systems II:

Strategic Workforce Planning, the Early Identification and Development of Executive Talent, and Succession Management

Chapter 4 focused on several high-impact organizational applications for career paths, including recruitment, hiring, retention, promotion, and employee development. This chapter builds on that discussion to address the role of career paths in workforce planning, the identification and development of high potentials, and succession management.

Keeping an Eye on the Big Picture

As stressed throughout this book, career paths should be developed with a clear purpose. Without question, a key reason for developing career paths in many organizations is to support the strategic direction of the organization. Almost every company has an overall vision or mission that serves as a focal point for resource allocation, prioritization, and development strategies. Most organizations also articulate strategic priorities and goals that define the organization's focus in the near term (i.e., within five years or less). Typically, senior leaders have overall responsibility and ownership for strategic priorities and goals but, ideally, those priorities and goals are cascaded throughout the organization, and all employees feel a sense of responsibility for helping the organization attain the goals.

Company strategies, visions, priorities, and goals really only gain traction throughout the organization when they are linked to and integrated with "people systems." Just look at any list of companies signified as great places to work (for example, Fortune's 100 Best Companies to Work For[1]). Companies like Google, Whole Foods, and Quicken succeed at attracting, developing, and retaining talent not only because they offer competitive pay and perks, but also because such companies offer employees new opportunities to build resumes, try new things, and move beyond current job responsibilities. Such successful companies create a sustainable and competitive advantage in part by providing rewarding career paths and substantive career opportunities to employees. Importantly, they also ensure that those career paths and opportunities are directly linked to corporate strategic priorities.

Consider our case example of EPC, Inc. discussed in Chapter 1. A move to increased global marketing and international presence opened up, or re-created, management and leadership career paths and to some extent changed the constituent competencies and experiences that were optimal for success. By making the link between the company's international expansion strategy and the career opportunities the strategy brought with it obvious through its career paths, EPC, Inc. ensured that its employees understood the implications of the strategy for their career development, and thus greatly increased the chances that the strategy would succeed.

Strategic Workforce Planning

Strategic workforce planning entails forecasting the number of people with specific competency profiles who will be needed in the future to successfully carry out the organization's overall strategy, and developing plans for dealing with anticipated shortages and overages. Steps involved in strategic workforce planning typically include:

- carefully examining the organization's overall strategy and deter-mining the human capital implications of that strategy;
- identifying the number of people with specific competency profiles who will be needed in the future to successfully execute the organi-zation's overall strategy;
- identifying the number of people with those profiles available in the organization today and the number of those people expected to be available at a specific future time (given specified assumptions regarding attrition due to retirement and other factors);
- identifying anticipated future personnel gaps/overages based on that analysis;
- developing specific plans for filling anticipated gaps and for pre-venting overages; and
- feeding back the results into the organization's broader strategic planning process.[2]

Conducting strategic workforce planning is more important today than ever. Baby Boomers are retiring with greater frequency and younger workers are more mobile than ever. Organizations that fail to plan appropriately increasingly find themselves faced with a daunt-ing gap between their leadership talent needs and talent available inside the organization.[3]

   Career paths that are directly linked to the strategic priorities of the organization (as discussed in the previous section) can be a very useful tool in conducting strategic workforce planning. You can use them to identify the specific competency portfolios that will be needed given the strategic direction of the company, and the nature and extent of the employee development that will need to occur to ensure that current employees attain the competency portfolios that will be needed in the future. If you intend to use your organization's career paths as an input into strategic workforce planning, it can be very useful to include information about the current and anticipated number of positions that exist/will exist in the future for each job, role, or level represented in the paths.

   Many organizations use a model or analytic tool to help guide their evaluation of "what they have" relative to "what they need" and, most importantly, "what they will need" as part of the strategic plan-ning process. In Chapter 3, we briefly discussed Internal Labor Market (ILM) analysis methods that were described by Haig Nalbantian and his colleagues.[4] These analysis methods and, more importantly, the overall strategic human capital model discussed in the book *Play to Your Strengths*,[5] provide a valuable approach for conducting strategic workforce planning and for ensuring that your organization's talent management system is closely and effectively tied to its overall corporate strategy. Career paths that are designed with the organization's strategic priorities in mind can be very useful when applying this approach. For example, Nalbantian and his colleagues point out that an organization's workforce, at any point in time, is the outcome of the three labor flows described in the box below.

Three Labor Flows from *Play to Your Strengths*

1. Attraction – how successful is the organization at attracting the kinds of people it needs to achieve its goals?
2. Development – how successful is it at growing and nurturing the kinds of human capital it needs to execute its business strategy?
3. Retention – how successful is it at retaining people who have the right capabilities and produce the highest value?

Source: Nalbantian et al. (2004)

The model and tools presented in *Play to Your Strengths* enable the organization to analyze these flows and gain a new and informed perspective on what it actually does with its workforce. The outputs of such an analysis can then be used to evaluate the organization's readiness, from a workforce perspective, to achieve its intended business outcomes. We can easily see how career paths are relevant to this analysis. Career path information can be used in the context of this analysis to inform judgments regarding any of the following issues:

1. whether the sequential linkages between roles support the current and future direction of the company;
2. whether there is alignment between hiring criteria and organizational criteria for success (e.g., whether needed qualifications are evaluated as part of the hiring process);
3. whether the available developmental experiences/training courses are adequate to facilitate movement along the paths;

4. whether there are gaps between what the company espouses and what it rewards in the form of career success factors.

Linking career paths to corporate strategy and using career path information in the strategic workforce planning process will ensure that the career paths you develop are ingrained into the organization and become a defining feature of its overall talent management system.

Identifying and Developing Early-Career, High-Potential Leadership Talent

Certain individuals merit a "fast track" approach along the career paths. By identifying individuals with high potential early and putting them on a "fast track" their value to the organization over the long run can increase exponentially. Moreover, employees placed in a fast track program may show an increase in their responsiveness to development and an increase in their motivation to lead. In addition, placing employees with outstanding potential in a high-potential program can improve retention of these people, resulting in decreased costs in recruiting, hiring, and training associated with replacing talent that leaves your organization.

You can use career paths that you design for your general employee population with high potentials, or you can develop career paths specifically for use with high-potential employees. If you do the latter, you can include jobs or roles in the paths for which there are relatively few openings, since you are dealing with a much smaller population than if you were designing paths for the general employee population. In addition, the paths will likely reflect more movement over a shorter period of time, and a more concentrated development focus than they would if you were developing the paths for the general employee population.

In this section, we focus on criteria for identifying high potentials, links to career paths, and options for accelerating high potentials within your organization.

Who Are Our High Potentials?

Many approaches to identifying high potentials exist, along with many myths about how to do so effectively. We present a few common myths regarding high potentials below.

Myth 1: Our highest performers are, by definition, our high potentials. Many organizations believe, mistakenly in our opinion, that high-performing employees are high-potential employees simply by virtue of their performance level. We suggest that high performance is a precursor to consideration as a high potential. Performance describes an employee's level of success in a current role while potential describes possible future success. An individual might be a high performer in a specific role and well placed in that role, and therefore not a high potential. An employee struggling in a role cannot be thought of as a high potential until he or she improves markedly in that role or demonstrates success in an alternate position.

Myth 2: Traits and personal attributes are irrelevant if the high potential employee has a strong track record. Not quite. In some cases, attributes that enable success at one level in the organization can inhibit success in a higher-level or alternative role. Organizations should strongly consider measuring personal attributes when examining who their high potentials might be. The employee who excels as a supervisor in an operational environment might easily behave as a micromanager when asked to lead across functional units. Further, if he or she isn't open to feedback and coaching from others, prospects for change and growth are dim.

Myth 3: High potentials must be identified early in their careers or it's too late. Certainly, there is the potential for maximum growth and return when younger workers are tagged as high potentials. Obviously, their career horizons are longer. Also, they are likely to be more open to alternative views and ways of operating beyond their own. However, those facts do not preclude organizations from considering the promise of mid-career, or even late career, individuals who might be willing and able to take on a set of challenges outside the work they've done for many years.

Organizations tend to rely on some combination of the criteria in the box on page 97 for identifying high potentials.[6]

For example, suppose EPC, Inc. decides to implement a high-potential leadership program to support its growth. The company will want to identify people at the Individual Contributor level with the potential to develop quickly into successful leaders. Without question, several of the types of criteria summarized in "Common Criteria for Identifying High Potentials" will be relied upon to help identify those employees most likely to "rise to the top." EPC, Inc.

Common Criteria for Identifying High Potentials

- Education requirements
- Tenure – role type, organization, industry
- Performance track record
- Leadership experience
- Specific technical skills
- Willingness to relocate
- Motivation to lead
- Demonstrated, adaptable interpersonal skills
- Strong, continuous learner
- Demonstrated openness to feedback and coaching from others

should carefully identify the most relevant criteria based on the success factors for leaders in the organization that it has identified and the competencies and qualifications for leadership roles specified in EPC, Inc.'s career paths. These criteria should then be communicated to leaders, the HR department, and others in the organization who are responsible for spotting talent. EPC, Inc.'s career paths can then be used to guide the rapid development of talented future leaders.

Regardless of the criteria chosen, the key to effectively aligning high-potential programs with career paths is to apply the criteria consistently. Nothing torpedoes a program of this kind in an organization more quickly than the perception, or worse yet, the reality that the criteria for identification as a high potential are subjective and/or applied inconsistently. Employees will only seriously incorporate considerations regarding how they can meet these criteria into their career decisions and development planning if they have seen consistency and follow-through within the organization. We recommend that you confer with your organization's HR and legal departments when establishing criteria and processes for identifying and selecting candidates for high-potential programs.

How Can We Develop (and Promote) Them Faster?

Of course, the ultimate goal of a high-potential (hi-po) program is to accelerate the development and advancement of talent as quickly as possible. Career paths can be valuable in doing this. Like any employee, high potentials should identify development targets using career path information and create an actionable development plan. The manager and/or mentor should guide the employee to identify the highest-return development activities (at the intersection of Business/Role/Self – see Chapter 4) to ensure rapid movement along one or more paths. Career path information is a critical tool in focusing the high-potential employee's planning.

When the organization reviews the progress of high potentials with an eye toward filling one or more openings, career path information is again relevant. The decision-making process can be much more accurate and efficient when the paths to the open role are clear and the progress of individuals along those paths has been tracked and documented.

Managing Communications Regarding High Potentials

Organizations must carefully consider how to manage communications regarding its high-potential program. Organizations need to ensure that high-potential employees know that they have strong career prospects in the organization and are guided toward continued, and often new levels of, success within the organization. Too often, a talented individual will leave an organization only to find, too late, that he or she was considered to be a key player or high potential for the future – but was never told of this status. However, organizations must also be careful not to de-motivate the large majority of the employee population that is not designated "high potential." Organizations that designate a group, or "pool," of high potentials have to think carefully about how to communicate with and about this group of critically important individuals. Figure 5.1 presents several characteristics describing how organizations choose to manage communications with and about high potentials. Each characteristic can be seen as a continuum; typically, organizations make compromises that result in a position somewhere between the end-points.

Ultimately, your organization should make decisions about positioning and managing high-potential programs in a way that best fits with its structure, business model, and cultural characteristics. However, it should be kept in mind that to use career paths to maximal advantage to develop high potentials, there needs to be

The program and its membership are **public**	The program and its membership are **secret**
High potentials **know** they are considered as such	High potentials **do not know** they are considered as such
Employees can **self-nominate**	Employees must be **nominated by others**
Criteria for being considered a hi-po are **known**	**Criteria** for being considered a hi-po are **unknown** in the broader organization
The program is used as a **recruiting/retention** tool	The program is **limited** in its application

Figure 5.1 Communicating With and About High Potentials

some degree of transparency in communications regarding the high-potential program, so that managers can freely discuss the career path and development implications of being designated a high-potential employee with employees who have been designated as such.

Succession Management

Succession management is the process used by an organization to identify employees for higher-level roles and develop those employees so that they are ready to take on those roles at the appropriate time. Traditionally, succession management has focused on a few critical leadership roles. Recently, however, organizations have begun to extend their succession management programs to a broader range of jobs. Career paths can be used both in identifying potential candidates for future roles (including, but not necessarily limited to, high-level leadership roles) and in developing those candidates. Most of the information included in this chapter and in Chapter 4 (including the information regarding career path applications to promotion, employee development, high-potential programs, etc.) is relevant to succession management.

As with a high-potential program, if you develop career paths specifically for succession management purposes, you should include jobs or roles in the paths for which there are relatively few openings if you are using the paths to guide the identification and development of candidates for those jobs/roles. In addition, as with career paths used for strategic workforce planning, it can be very useful to include information about the current and anticipated number of positions that exist/will exist in the future for each job, role, or level represented in paths that are designed for use in a succession management context.

Prior to defining a succession management strategy, an organization should follow the steps outlined in the box below.

Steps to Follow Prior to Developing a Succession Management Strategy

1. Confirm the need for, and the means to develop, career paths for the organization.
2. Establish the purpose for paths in the organization.
3. Confirm that jobs and roles are clearly defined through job analyses, position descriptions, etc.
4. Develop career paths that include critical leadership roles using the procedures described in Chapter 3.
5. Conduct an organization-level analysis to identify talent needs and gaps (see strategic workforce planning discussion).
6. Ensure that a supportive employee development environment exists.
7. Establish and manage an ongoing program for moving employees along one or more career paths.

Once talent needs and the talent gap are known, organizations must take steps to address the gap for both the current state and the future. Organizations can essentially follow their career paths in reverse from the highest-level positions to the entry level. Along the way, they should identify where their relative bench strength is strong, adequate, or insufficient.

So, EPC, Inc. should start this effort with their Senior Leader roles, both current and projected, to identify the number of ready leaders the company will need in order to achieve its expansion and growth goals. Assume that the company has identified how many international Division General Managers will be needed based on the number of locations that will be opened. Several other questions follow:

- How many Business Managers are needed?
- Knowing that many future leaders will come from within, how many General Managers will need to be replaced because they are promoted to Vice President positions?
- What will this growth effort mean for Vice Presidents and other leaders?

Finally, increased recruiting efforts might be needed to ensure that the pipeline of Individual Contributors is replenished to support ongoing growth. Career paths will help drive the analysis, decision-making, and resulting talent movement associated with these critical questions.

Evaluating Readiness for Promotion in the Context of Succession Management

The highest expectations in a succession management scenario are placed upon high potentials. By definition, these individuals are expected to be both motivated and able to "get there sooner." Development plans for hi-pos should reflect the optimal movement patterns to satisfy the organization and the individual (per our Business/Role/Self discussion in Chapter 4). From an organizational perspective, a naturally occurring question at this point is – "Who is ready to move ahead in the organization?" While this question is important at every level of the organization, it is critically important as we move higher in the organizational hierarchy. The decision of whether or not Joe is ready to move from Sales Coordinator to Account Manager is an important one. The decision of whether or not Mary is the right person to become a General Manager and lead our company's expansion in Asia is critical. So, how do we make promotion decisions that are loaded with risk?

The evaluation process underlying promotion decisions is complex and delicate when making decisions about critical positions. Having all of your "tickets punched" does not guarantee success at the next level. As discussed earlier in this chapter, demonstrated past performance and potential for the next level are different things and they require different assessment approaches. Not all organizations can embrace robust, resource intensive, relatively expensive assessments to evaluate the readiness of their talent. However, they should consider the risk of making the wrong decision and gather and use as much decision information as budgets and the organizational environment support.

Methods for Evaluating Readiness

As noted earlier, readiness can be evaluated using any of a number of approaches and tools. These approaches vary by complexity, cost, and time. Several examples are presented in the box on page 103. While not mutually exclusive, each represents a common approach to evaluating readiness.

Job requirements are typically considered the target criteria against which to evaluate an employee's readiness. For example, a high-potential General Manager (GM) at EPC, Inc. might be evaluated against the job requirements for a Vice President role. The organization can measure the GM candidate's readiness based on qualifications, experiences, job knowledge, and competencies. If the employee is judged to be "not yet ready" then career path information can be used to identify the best means to get there. Career path information can also be used to identify alternative career options for employees who are not considered viable candidates for a certain job. Perhaps the employee is talented and valuable but might never rise to the role in question. Career path information can inform discussions regarding other options for future roles and thus can help in retaining this employee.

Keeping Those "Not Yet Ready" on the Path(s) to Get There

So, what happens to employees who are not chosen for promotion or special development activities at a given point in time? How do you keep them motivated? How do you avoid losing valuable employees who are just not quite ready yet, especially when they think they are ready? As with many other scenarios, career paths can help. Let's illustrate this point with a story (see box on page 104).

Common Methods for Evaluating Readiness for Promotion in the Context of Succession Management

Sequence and time in roles

Employees are sometimes considered ready for a move by virtue of the time spent in role. This evaluation is often extended to the sequence of roles. For example, an Accountant I typically progresses to Accountant II after a certain amount of time. Non-linear role changes often require additional information as the organization cannot assume that the requisite skills, knowledge, and experiences have been gained in the previous role.

Technical training and expertise

Eligibility for advancement can be achieved by gaining specific skills training and expertise inside and/or outside of the organization. Time is not the driving factor here – employees are likely to progress at differential rates. This option often includes a knowledge test, certification process, or other "gate" to the next level.

High potential with promise

Less commonly, a standout hi-po will be advanced based on his/her "promise" – typically defined as early career success across a number of challenges and situations. This evaluation is akin to the "best available athlete" decision-making often employed in drafting players in sports leagues.

Broad development portfolio

The most attractive option in some situations might be the person with the broadest background. Rather than relying on deep expertise and experience in a specific area, organizations sometimes rely on an individual who has held varied roles and gained broad experience and knowledge.

Simulation-based assessment

Individuals can be given the opportunity to "try on" the role for which they are being considered. For example, a manager might spend the day simulating the role of a Vice President, presented with a series of goals, challenges, and role-play interactions that approximate the VP role in the company. The manager's performance is then evaluated against the criteria for the Vice President role, providing an estimate of the manager's readiness to step up to that level.

The Story of Todd and Bill

Todd and Bill join the company

Todd joined a consumer products company as a software designer and programmer. Todd had been out of college for a few years and had worked as a contract programmer at a few companies.

Bill joined the same company at about the same time as Todd in a similar role. Bill is younger than Todd and had some limited experience in the IT industry.

Early career at the company

As the company's business grew rapidly, so too did its reliance on in-house IT capability. Bill was given a team leadership role and he managed a group of ten programmers for both product development and client services. His reputation grew as a smart, gun-slinger type who made risky decisions that sometimes paid off and sometimes did not.

Todd remained as an Individual Contributor, moving through a number of focus areas in his role, including R&D, client service, platform integration, and growth of the infrastructure. His reputation grew as that of a quietly confident resource who made solid decisions on a consistent basis.

Early leadership opportunities

As growth continued, both Bill and Todd ascended to Director-level leadership roles. They both reported to the VP of Consumer Technology and each managed multiple teams within the department. At this point, each had been with the company for five to six years.

The winds of change blow in

After nearly four years in their tenures as Directors, Todd's and Bill's boss (the VP) abruptly left the company. Although a few other candidates emerged, all agreed that either Todd or Bill would be the likely successor. After an assessment process, Todd was named as the new VP. Although similar in tenure, background, and experience at the company, Todd outperformed Bill in the assessment and emerged as the more solid choice to lead the group into the future.

What about Bill?

Although Todd was promoted and Bill was not, Bill remains a very important piece of the company's future. His leadership and expertise are essential to Todd's success and the success of the Consumer Technology group as a whole. Bill thought he would be promoted to the VP role and now wonders what the future holds for him at the company.

Obviously, the company needs to handle Bill carefully at this time. His ego is bruised, and he wonders what is missing from his portfolio that prevented him from being promoted. The company must carefully and clearly lay out the rationale for its decision. Moreover, Bill should understand exactly where he fell short against the required experiences, skills, or competencies. Career path information can be very useful in helping Bill to understand where he fell short. Bill's manager and/or coach should also speak with Bill about his career opportunities. Career path information will obviously be useful in this discussion. Bill might be well served to stay on the path he has traveled thus far, or he might be better served by a shift to an adjacent or alternative path. After helping Bill to understand his near- and long-term options, Bill should receive significant development support to close any competency or experience gaps that could hinder his future progression. In the end, there is no guarantee that Bill will not leave the organization, but these steps can certainly help to increase his connection to the company.

The Bottom Line

In this chapter and in Chapter 4, we described how career paths can be integrated into a number of important components of your organization's overall talent management system. As we discussed, career paths serve a very important role in each of these components. However, the significance of the role of career paths in these individual system components pales in comparison to the significance of their role as a mechanism for linking these components together into a cohesive and seamless structure. This linkage will provide a real competitive advantage to your organization.

Chapter 6

Expanding Success Beyond the Individual Organization – Industry and Economic Development Perspectives

Up to this point, this book has focused on how to develop career paths and use those paths to enhance the success of your organization and its employees. In this chapter, we show that career paths can not only help organizations succeed – they can also help entire industries succeed and geographic regions prosper.

At this point you are probably thinking "Come on, get real. Are you saying career paths are the answer to all of the world's economic problems?" Of course not. But, as we'll show in this chapter, we are saying that career paths can be used – and are being used – to promote industries, the awareness of career opportunities within industries, and awareness of the career preparation needed to succeed in specific industries. Moreover, career paths and associated tools and resources are being used to cultivate knowledge workers in ways that are targeted toward the needs and potential of populations in specific geographic regions. By doing these things, career path information used in the context of coherent and coordinated industry and economic development strategies can positively influence the success and prosperity of industries and geographic regions. In fact, we'll go even further than that and say that this information can in turn help to maintain national economic vitality within the quickly changing global economy.

We begin this chapter by defining "the industry perspective" and "the economic development perspective." Then, we describe the uses of career paths by industries. Next, we describe the application of career paths and associated tools and resources to enhance regional economic development. Finally, we discuss how labor market analyses can be used to project labor supply and demand in jobs, industries, and occupations, and how analyses of competency requirements across occupations can be used to develop cross-occupation career paths and to identify potential labor markets for industries and opportunities for employees in declining industries.

The industry perspective is the perspective of persons who represent the interests and views of an entire industry or industry sector, as opposed to an individual organization within an industry. One or more industry associations represent almost every industry – there are undoubtedly associations representing your industry. These associations are funded by individual organizations with economic interests in the industry, and promote the interests of the industry through various means including public outreach, media relations, training, and government relations activities (often including lobbying). In addition, virtually every profession has established one or more professional associations. Professional associations are made up of individuals who are in a particular profession, and the associations exist to serve the needs of individual members. An example of a professional association is the Society for Human Resource Management, or SHRM. As will be discussed in this chapter, many industry associations and professional associations provide information to the public about careers and career opportunities in the industries or professions they represent, and some of these associations have worked with their member organizations or individual members (perhaps including you or others in your organization) to develop career paths.

For purposes of this book, the economic development perspective can be viewed broadly as the collective perspective of government, industry, and educational entities that form partnerships to enhance regional economic development and employment opportunities. There are many organizations, programs, and initiatives that have been established to enhance regional economic development in the United States. For example, the Economic Development Administration, which is the Department of Commerce's domestic economic arm, was formed to generate jobs, help to ensure that existing jobs are retained, and stimulate economic and commercial growth in economically distressed areas within the United States.[1] Economic development entities have recognized the value of career paths that show the specific linkages between vocational preparation and career opportunities in enhancing workforce readiness and economic opportunity.

While industry associations are focused on the interests of their member organizations and economic development organizations are focused on the economic interests of a region, these two perspectives are closely linked and have much in common. In fact, industry associations are frequently active participants in economic development initiatives and some industry association websites provide information about economic development initiatives that are relevant to their members.

Career Paths and the Industry Perspective

Career paths have several useful functions from an industry perspective. First, they can be used to encourage people to enter an industry or profession by making them aware of the range of career opportunities within the industry, by presenting entry-level positions in the industry as starting points on a fulfilling career journey as opposed to dead-end jobs, and by providing information about how to pursue a career in the industry. For an industry to thrive, the companies that comprise the industry – including your company – must be able to attract and retain a sufficient number of employees who have specific portfolios of qualifications and skills or who have the potential to obtain those portfolios of qualifications and skills. A shortage of qualified labor can have a serious detrimental impact on an industry and can be devastating to an individual corporation. In many sectors of the economy, there is fierce competition for highly skilled employees and high-potential employees. Readily accessible information about career paths can provide an advantage to your industry and to your organization in that talent competition.

Second, by providing information about the qualifications (such as training, education, certifications, licenses, and experience) and competencies required for various jobs and roles within an industry or profession, career paths can be used by individuals to identify industries and careers for which they may be suited. By educating people about career prospects and job requirements, they can serve a valuable role in matching individuals with industries, occupations, and jobs for which they are suited and steering them away from industries, occupations, and jobs for which they are not suited.

Third, and closely related to the other two functions, career paths can show people the specific, concrete steps they can take to enter an industry or profession. This includes the training, education, or other career preparation they should pursue if they aspire to a career in the industry or profession. In some cases, web-based career path resources even contain links to job listings. This is extremely valuable because it provides a direct connection between the jobs or roles shown on the career paths and real career opportunities, and it can quickly produce informed and qualified applicants for jobs within an industry.

Industry and professional associations, in general, understand the importance of disseminating information to the public about careers and career opportunities, and many of these associations provide some form of career information to the public. The extent and specific nature of this information varies widely. In some cases, it includes career paths highlighting career opportunities in the relevant industry or profession.

Examples

The NRF Foundation (the research and education arm of the National Retail Federation) developed a set of Career Profiles that provide information about the career paths and career insights of individuals in the retail industry. These Career Profiles are available on the National Retail Federation's website (www.nrf.com/retailcareers). Figure 6.1 shows the NRF Foundation Career Profile for Kathi, the Senior Vice President and General Manager of the Retail Division of an international specialty store chain.

The Home Builders Institute (HBI) is the workforce development arm of the National Association of Home Builders. As noted in Chapter 3, HBI undertook an initiative, labeled the Careers Campaign, to improve the home building industry's image, to promote careers in the industry, and to encourage people to consider careers in the home building industry. The website for the initiative (www.building-careers.org) provides information about careers in the residential

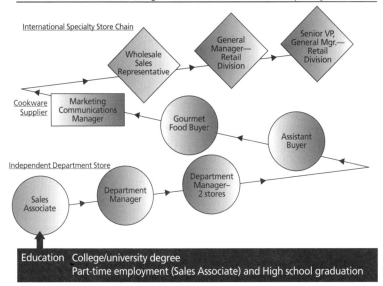

Figure 6.1 NRF Foundation Career Profile

Source: National Retail Federation

(http://www.nrf.com/retailcareers/); used with permission.

 NRF FOUNDATION
RESEARCH & EDUCATION

 Store Operations

Name: **Kathi** Title: **Senior VP and General Manager, Retail Division**
Company: **International Specialty Store Chain**

This is a description of Kathi's career path from her high school years through December 12, 2001

Career Path

EDUCATION • EDUCATION • EDUCATION • EDUCATION

EDUCATION

Part-time employment – Sales Associate
↓
High school graduation
↓
College/University Degree: Journalism
↓

> *Kathi ended up in retail right out of college. She wasn't able to get a job right away in journalism because she didn't have any experience. So, she began working in a family-owned department store, thinking she would stay there unitil she got a job in her field. But she was promoted for her good work and decided to stay.*

FULL TIME EMPLOYMENT • FULL TIME EMPLOYMENT

FULL TIME EMPLOYMENT

Independent Department Store
▪ Sales Associate
↓
■ Department Manager
↓
■ Department Manager–2 stores
↓
■ Assistant Buyer
↓
■ Gourmet Food Buyer
↓

> *Kathi's upward progression at the department store gave her opportunities to build her knowledge and skills. As Gourmet Food Buyer, she knew the cookware department's products inside and out. As a result, the store's biggest cookware supplier recruited her to their company, where Kathi was in charge of the company's recipes, magazine, and testing program.*

Cookware Supplier
■ Marketing Communications Manager
↓

> *At the cookware supplier, Kathi was in charge of the company's recipes, magazine, and testing program.*

CONTINUED

Figure 6.1 NRF Foundation Career Profile

NRF FOUNDATION
RESEARCH & EDUCATION

Learn more @ ——— www.nrf.com/RetailCareers

RETAIL CAREERS
&ADVANCEMENT

Retail
Career
Profiles

Store Operations

Name: **Kathi**   Title: **Senior VP and General Manager, Retail Division**
Company: **International Specialty Store Chain**

This is a description of Kathi's career path from her high school years through December 12, 2001

Career Snapshot (cont.)

Full time employment • full time employment (cont.)

International Specialty Store Chain

▪ Wholesale Sales Representative
   ↓
▪ General Manager–Retail Division
   ↓
▪ Senior Vice President and General Manger, Retail Division

FULL TIME EMPLOYMENT

> Then, Kathi joined an International Specialty Store Chain, which was
> the second largest vendor at her original department store. She became
> the Wholesale Sales Representative, selling to department store buyers
> in stores like the one in which she began her career. Kathi was successful
> in this position because she had retail experience...she knew the buyers'
> business and could understand and address their needs. She has been
> promoted several times at this company.

‣ CAREER SNAPSHOT

Figure 6.1 NRF Foundation Career Profile

 NRF FOUNDATION
RESEARCH & EDUCATION

 Retail Career Profiles

Store Operations

Name: **Kathi**   Title: **Senior VP and General Manager, Retail Division**
Company: **International Specialty Store Chain**

◄ CAREER PATH   *This is a description of Kathi's career path from her high school years through December 12, 2001*

Career Snapshot

CAREER INSIGHT

COMPENSATION AND EXPERIENCE

First wage/salary
$2.25 per hour in 1971 as a part-time gift wrapper in a department store.

Current salary
Over $100,000 annually.

Employer-provided benefits
Health, dental, and life insurance; 401K and retirement plan; stock options; 4 weeks vacation

Years in retail 25 years

The education–career connection:
College was critical to help Kathi focus on her skills. Her degree in journalism gave her the ability to write well, which has been important in managing the Retail Division of the International Specialty Store Chain.
Most important academic skills Marketing Education/DECA program, English courses
Most important soft/life skills   Appreciation for people, great interpersonal skills

Experience (s) that have contributed to career success
Rising from the retail ranks–knowing the business from the ground up.

Personal traits that have contributed to career success
Enterpreneurial spirit and a "can do" attitude.

WHAT IT'S LIKE

Typical work schedule Monday–Friday 8:00 AM–6:30/7:00 PM, Kathi works in an office building, Her responsibilities include a lot of phone, e-mail, and written correspondence with other corporate executives and her retail sales team. She evaluates sales figures and identifies future goals based on current company performance. She also travels to stores and meetings, about 3 to 5 days per month.

You'd like my job if you like an environment that is..
"...fast-paced, with something new happening every day. I'm doing a variety of things every day, so I must be flexible, stay organized, and set priorities daily."

CONTINUED

Figure 6.1 NRF Foundation Career Profile

Learn more @
www.nrf.com/RetailCareers

Store Operations

Name: **Kathi**   Title: **Senior VP and General Manager, Retail Division**
Company: **International Specialty Store Chain**

This is a description of Kathi's career path from her high school years through December 12, 2001

Career Snapshot (cont.)

CAREER INSIGHT

WHAT IT'S LIKE (cont.)

Most satisfying aspect of career
People–building an organization of people dedicated to pursing and achieving common goals.

Most challenging aspect of career
Being the only "retailer" on the management team.

ASPIRATIONS and ADVICE

Why retail?
Even as a young person, Kathi was a good salesperson, with an entrepreneurial spirit and a "can do" attitude. She sold the most Girl Scout cookies in Tulsa, Oklahoma using a then seldom employed method–telemarketing.

In 5 years...
Kathi reports retailing is an exciting place to be; she really enjoys running a luxury retail business. She plans to say involved in this type of retailing.

Advice to career seekers
"Don't overlook retail as a great career opportunity. I've learned it isn't something to do while you're waiting for another opportunity. There is a retail business for every interest. It's a great job and a career path that can lead to exciting opportunities, challenges, and a lucrative career path."

Figure 6.1 NRF Foundation Career Profile

construction industry. Figure 6.2 shows a career path diagram available on that website. The diagram is designed to be used in conjunction with more detailed information about career options in the residential construction industry that is also available on the website.

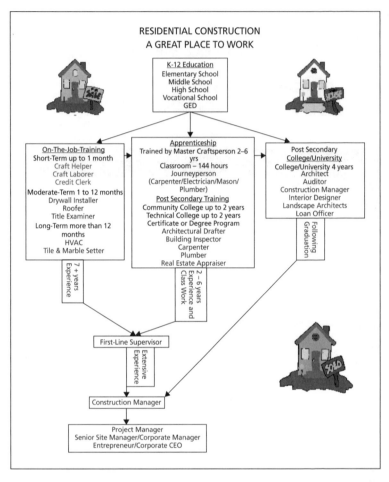

Figure 6.2 Home Builders Institute Residential Construction Career Path Model

Source: Home Builders Institute (http://www.buildingcareers.org); used with permission.

Differences between Industry Career Paths and Organizational Career Paths

As stressed throughout this book, career paths should be purpose driven. Thus, it makes sense that there would be some differences between the career paths designed for an individual organization and those designed for an entire industry. But exactly how do they differ? In many ways they are similar and you can implement the same step-by-step process we described in Chapter 3 for developing career paths for organizations if you are developing career paths for an industry. The main differences are that industry paths are designed to show opportunities spanning many organizations rather than a single organization, and that the target population includes not only those already in the organization but also (often primarily) people whom you are trying to attract to the industry. These differences should be reflected both in the sources that you use to develop the paths and in the specific information that you include in the paths.

Information used in developing industry career paths should cut across organizations within the industry. Thus, interviews and focus groups should be held with representatives of a number of organizations employing persons in the industry rather than with representatives of a single organization. If you are using information from surveys, the surveys should include information from people representing a number of organizations (preferably a representative sample of organizations) in the industry. If you are deriving career path information using analyses of existing data, the data should not be HR data from a single organization. Instead, the data should be from many organizations. For this reason, publicly available information such as information in O*NET and salary and employment projections available from the U.S. Department of Labor's Bureau of Labor Statistics can be even more valuable when you are developing career paths for your industry than it is when you are developing career paths for a single organization because it is statistically representative of entire occupations or industries. Your industry association may also gather and maintain data that you can use when developing career paths.

Just as the sources that you use to obtain industry career path information should cut across organizations that are part of the industry, the information that is included in the paths should also be relevant across organizations. For example, qualifications should be those required to succeed in the industry as a whole or in occupations comprising the industry. Qualifications idiosyncratic to a single organization should not be included. Similarly, critical developmental experiences should be relevant across organizations and thus will tend to be more general than those developed for a single organization. Career success factors should be factors important in the industry rather than in a particular organization, and may include, for example, interests and educational or experiential backgrounds of persons who tend to succeed in the industry.

Because an important part of the target population is people whom you are trying to attract to the industry, information about career preparation needed to enter the occupations represented in the industry should generally be included in industry career paths. Moreover, in many cases it will be helpful to include other information that people considering career options commonly want to know. As noted above, this includes salary information and employment projections. As discussed in Chapter 3, salary information (including mean and median wages) and employment projections by occupation and industry are available on the U.S. Department of Labor's Bureau of Labor Statistics website (http://www.bls.gov/).

Career Paths and the Economic Development Perspective

Economic trends, including the emergence of a global economy and the increasing importance of highly skilled labor to successfully compete in that economy, have resulted in an increasing need to put mechanisms in place to enable and encourage the cultivation and continuing enhancement of marketable knowledge and skills. Davis Jenkins[2] notes that the two factors most important to economic development are "… a working population capable of earning family-supporting wages, and a thriving, technology-intensive industry base" (p. 3), and argues that whether geographic regions within the United States thrive or decline will be driven in large part by how well they cultivate knowledge workers.

For several reasons, career paths can play a significant role in cultivating knowledge workers and thus promoting economic development. First, they provide valuable information for individuals to use in ensuring that their educational and career decisions will result in fulfilling careers in occupations where there is a reasonable probability of achieving their economic aspirations. This can include both information about which occupations and skills are in high demand (nationally or in a geographic region) and information about concrete steps that people can take to achieve their career goals. Second, as discussed extensively in this book, career paths are valuable work-force development tools, and you can customize them to address regional corporate or industry needs and opportunities (e.g., based on the skills base of a population in a given area and the type of business operations that exist in a region). Third, career paths can be valuable curriculum planning and career guidance tools for educational institutions (particularly community colleges) because they provide information about training, education, and competency requirements for employment in general, and for employment in high-demand industries and occupations in particular. Finally, and most importantly, they can be used as mechanisms to align the efforts of educational institutions, businesses, and public programs so that they work together to ensure that the workforce (and the future workforce) has the capabilities and information needed to succeed and consequently to ensure regional economic vitality. This alignment has direct and immediate benefits for your organization – it ensures that the workforce available to your organization has the skills your organization needs, both now and in the future.

Jenkins[3] describes a number of ways in which there is a lack of alignment among training and education systems and between these systems and the labor market. This lack of alignment stymies efforts to build regional knowledge workforces and has direct implications for the ability of your organization to successfully compete in the global marketplace. However, there is a growing realization of the long-term implications of this problem for regional economic development and for the ability of the United States to maintain a strong position in the global economy, and efforts are under way to address it. Jenkins states that, in a number of regions, "… local leaders are working to more closely coordinate publicly funded education, from primary through postsecondary levels, with social services and workforce and economic development programs to produce a better-trained workforce and promote economic development" (p. 6).

One important way in which this coordination is happening is through the application of the career pathways framework or approach. Jenkins and Jenkins and Spence[4] describe the career pathways framework as a means of building a knowledge workforce suited to local labor market needs. Jenkins[5] defines a career pathway as "… a series of connected education and training programs and support services that enable individuals to secure employment within a specific industry or occupational sector, and to advance over time to successively higher levels of education and employment in that sector" (p. 6). In a report published by the League for Innovation in the Community College,[6] Ashok Agrawal and colleagues state that the ultimate goal of efforts using the career pathways framework is "... for pathways to provide a seamless system of career exploration, preparation, and skill upgrades linked to academic credits and credentials, available with multiple entry and exit points spanning middle school, secondary school, postsecondary institutions, adult education, and workplace education" (p. 3).

There are three notable features of the career pathways framework that are hallmarks of the economic development perspective. First, the framework is designed to promote regional economic development. Second, the framework places a heavy emphasis on education and training. Third, the framework stresses the alignment among publicly supported programs (including education and training programs and support services) and between those programs and the labor market. Initiatives implementing the career pathways framework often identify training- and education-focused career paths (labeled career pathways) as part of their efforts.

Examples

Oregon's Pathways Statewide Initiative is an example of a program that implements the career pathways framework. All seventeen of Oregon's community colleges participate in this initiative, in partnership with Oregon's high school Career & Technical Education Network, Department of Education, Employment Department, Department of Human Services, and workforce investment boards.[7] The website for the initiative (http://www.worksourceoregon.org) contains links to over a hundred community college-oriented career pathways that address a broad array of career fields. In most cases, the information available through the initiative's website and/or through the websites for the participating colleges includes a summary diagram depicting a career pathway for a particular occupational area or field of study and detailed educational and occupational information such as information about course and certification requirements for specific jobs along the career pathway, average wages for jobs comprising the career pathway in relevant geographic areas, and links to current job announcements. Example diagrams providing information about career pathways designed and disseminated as part of this initiative are shown in Figures 6.3 and 6.4. Figure 6.3 shows a summary of a computer information systems career pathway designed

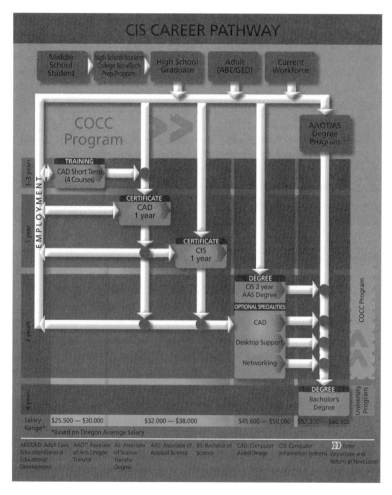

Figure 6.3 Central Oregon Community College Computer Information Systems Career Pathway

Source: Career pathway design by Darius Whitten; used with permission.

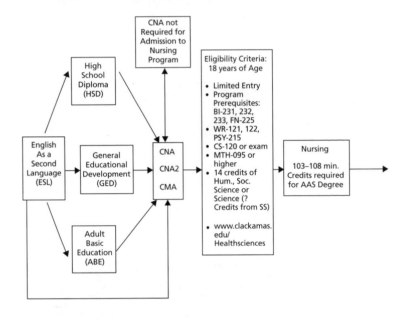

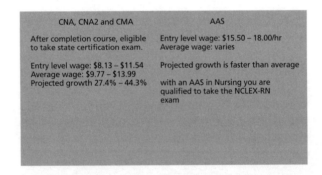

Figure 6.4 Clackamas Community College Nursing Pathway
Source: http://www2.clackamas.edu/pathways/viewCareer.asp?ClackamasOptionID=7&pathwayID=1; used with permission.

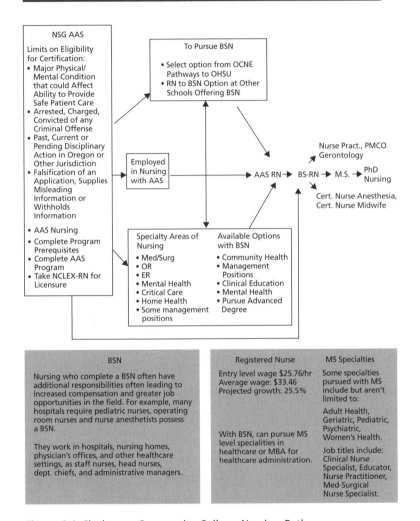

NSG AAS

Limits on Eligibility for Certification:
- Major Physical/ Mental Condition that could Affect Ability to Provide Safe Patient Care
- Arrested, Charged, Convicted of any Criminal Offense
- Past, Current or Pending Disciplinary Action in Oregon or Other Jurisdiction
- Falsification of an Application, Supplies Misleading Information or Withholds Information

- AAS Nursing
- Complete Program Prerequisites
- Complete AAS Program
- Take NCLEX-RN for Licensure

To Pursue BSN
- Select option from OCNE Pathways to OHSU
- RN to BSN Option at Other Schools Offering BSN

Employed in Nursing with AAS

AAS RN → BS-RN → M.S. → PhD Nursing

Nurse Pract., PMCO Gerontology

Cert. Nurse Anesthesia, Cert. Nurse Midwife

Specialty Areas of Nursing
- Med/Surg
- OR
- ER
- Mental Health
- Critical Care
- Home Health
- Some management positions

Available Options with BSN
- Community Health
- Management Positions
- Clinical Education
- Mental Health
- Pursue Advanced Degree

BSN

Nursing who complete a BSN often have additional responsibilities often leading to increased compensation and greater job opportunities in the field. For example, many hospitals require pediatric nurses, operating room nurses and nurse anesthetists possess a BSN.

They work in hospitals, nursing homes, physician's offices, and other healthcare settings, as staff nurses, head nurses, dept. chiefs, and administrative managers.

Registered Nurse

Entry level wage $25.76/hr
Average wage: $33.46
Projected growth: 25.5%

With BSN, can pursue MS level specialities in healthcare or MBA for healthcare administration.

MS Specialties

Some specialties pursued with MS include but aren't limited to:

Adult Health, Geriatric, Pediatric, Psychiatric, Women's Health.

Job titles include: Clinical Nurse Specialist, Educator, Nurse Practitioner, Med-Surgical Nurse Specialist.

Figure 6.4 Clackamas Community College Nursing Pathway

by Central Oregon Community College. Each node on the pathway is linked to a web page providing information about course requirements. Figure 6.4 shows a nursing career pathway developed by Clackamas Community College. It contains information about career options and specialties available in the field of nursing.

Differences between Career Paths Designed for Economic Development Purposes and Organizational Career Paths

Career paths designed for economic development purposes, including those developed as part of initiatives implementing the career pathways framework, have a different focus and end-goal than career paths designed for individual organizations, and therefore typically include somewhat different content. However, they also typically have several characteristics in common with those career paths, including the specification of a sequential series of positions or roles and the qualifications (particularly education and training requirements) associated with each. They also often include information about competency requirements for the positions identified in the paths.

If your organization participates in an effort to develop career paths as part of an economic development initiative, you can implement the same step-by-step process we described in Chapter 3 for developing career paths for organizations. However, there are three main differences between paths designed for economic development purposes and those designed for individual organizations, and those differences should be reflected in the process used to develop the paths. First, when identifying the occupations for which to develop paths, the focus is on occupations that hold the most promise for a particular geographic region. Thus, a variety of factors should be considered when selecting occupations upon which to focus that are different from those considered when identifying occupations for a career path project for an individual organization. These include, for example, the existing industry base in the region, natural resources, economic development goals, and the current skills of the local population. Second, just as with industry career path efforts, the sources that you use to obtain career path information designed for economic development purposes should cut across organizations, and the information that is included in the paths should be relevant across organizations. Finally, there should be a much heavier emphasis on career preparation when you are developing career paths for economic development purposes than there is when you are developing them for an individual organization. Specific and detailed information about education and training requirements should be a central focus – but not the only focus – of the paths.

Many of the paths that have been designed for economic development purposes in the past have included only information about career preparation – the education and training steps needed to obtain jobs in a career field. While this is appropriate in some circumstances, career paths designed for economic development purposes are generally more useful in aligning the efforts of educational institutions, businesses, and public programs when they include all five of the fundamental career path components stressed throughout this book.

Labor Market Analyses and Analyses of Cross-Occupation Requirements

Labor Market Analyses

As discussed in Chapter 3, statistical modeling techniques can be used to examine labor supply, the demand for labor, and employee movement across occupations, industries, or sectors of the economy. For example, many studies have been conducted to project the supply of physicians in the United States overall, by region, and by specialty. Studies have also been conducted to project the demand for physicians.[8] These types of studies can be useful in predicting potential shortages of qualified employees in a job or role at a specific point along a career path, in an occupation, in an industry, and/or in a region. They can also provide insight into the potential impact of various factors (such as salary level) on labor supply and the demand for labor. Armed with this information, corporations, industries, economic development organizations, and government officials can take steps to avoid potential labor shortages or overages. Steps to avoid shortages can include, for example, education grants to encourage students to enter specific fields, public outreach to promote industries or occupations, increases in employee training and development focused on specific skills predicted to be in short supply in the future, increased recruitment efforts by your organization and other individual organizations, and various economic development efforts focused on specific industries or occupations in targeted geographic regions.

Similarly, analyses can be conducted to identify "traffic patterns" of people through jobs and careers in an industry, and high-traffic "exit points," or points along careers at which there tends to be high attrition. You can then take steps to reduce attrition at those critical points.

Analyses of Requirements across Occupations

As noted in Chapter 1, career paths have become more varied and emergent as people make career decisions under increasingly dynamic circumstances. Many people change occupations several times over the course of their careers. In most circumstances, the occupations into which people move have occupational requirements that are at least somewhat similar to the requirements of their old occupations. In general, people tend not to move into occupations that are so different from their previous occupations that the knowledge, skills, abilities, and education required in the previous occupations are completely irrelevant to the new occupations. Moreover, if placed in circumstances in which we are forced to consider different occupations due to a lack of opportunity in an occupation as a result of changes in the global economy, most of us would be anxious to take full advantage of the knowledge and skills learned on a previous job to land a job in a different career field. Thus, to identify cross-occupation career opportunities and paths, it is useful to compare the requirements (skills, abilities, etc.) of occupations and identify those with similar requirements.

As discussed previously, O*NET, the web-based occupational information tool sponsored by the U.S. Department of Labor, contains a great deal of valuable information about most occupations in the U.S. economy. Information is gathered on the same variables, or descriptors, for all O*NET occupations. As a result, you can use O*NET data to compare requirements and characteristics across occupations and identify occupations with similar, and different, requirements. Such analyses can be used to develop cross-occupation career paths and to identify potential labor pools for jobs or roles for which there is a labor supply shortage in a region or industry.

There are at least two ways to identify occupations with similar requirements by using the O*NET website (http://online.onetcenter. org/). First, there is a skills search function in O*NET that allows you to find occupations requiring specific skills that you select from a skills list. You can use this function to find occupations with similar profiles of required skills. Second, when you go to a description of any O*NET occupation (either a summary report or a detailed report), a list of related occupations is provided. These lists are based on the level of similarity in ratings on O*NET knowledge, skill, ability, work context, and work activity variables.[9]

Analyses of requirements across occupations can also be used in identifying the extent to which specific skills are prevalent in a geographic region. For example, the Geo-Skills™ Profile (www.geoskillanalyzer.com) uses O*NET data combined with data from other sources, including the Bureau of Labor Statistics and the U.S. Census Bureau, to produce reports providing information about workforce characteristics in specific geographic areas. This information includes, for example, the number of incumbents in various industries and occupations in a specific geographic region, and estimates of the relative skill concentration in a specific geographic area compared to the concentration of the skill in the United States as a whole. This information can be used in the economic development context to develop cross-occupation career paths and to attract businesses and industries seeking employees with certain skills to a region.

The Bottom Line

Career path information can play an important role in promoting industries and enhancing regional economic opportunity, and can have a direct and immediate impact on the ability of your organization to maintain a pipeline of qualified applicants. Ultimately, however, the identification and dissemination of career path information by industries and economic developers can have an impact that extends beyond individual organizations, industries, or geographic regions. As stressed in this chapter, career paths can help to cultivate a knowledge workforce, attract people to high-demand industries and occupations, and serve as mechanisms to align efforts of educational institutions, businesses, and public programs so that they work together to ensure that the workforce has the capabilities and information needed to succeed. By serving these functions, career path information can help to maintain national economic vitality within the quickly changing global economy.

Chapter 7

Looking to the Future

Taking out a crystal ball and forecasting trends of future significance is always a risky proposition. However, this book would be incomplete without sharing a few predictions regarding how career path and talent management trends may take shape in the future. In Chapter 2, we briefly mentioned three career trends that currently affect organizational landscapes, namely:

1. less of a focus on linear career status and progress and a greater emphasis on personal interests and work–life balance;
2. a focus on developing transferable skills versus organization-specific skills; and
3. decreased loyalty to a specific organization versus broader professional commitment.

Other trends were also noted throughout the book. Here, we consolidate our thinking about a number of broader, macro-level trends that are likely to influence talent management in general, and career decisions and career paths in particular. Figure 7.1 provides an overview of these trends. Where possible, we highlight what you can do in anticipation of, or in reaction to, these trends to positively impact career decisions in your organization.

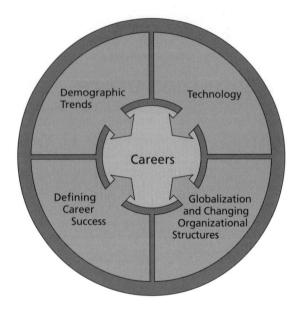

Figure 7.1 Macro-level Trends Impacting Talent Management

Trend One – Demographic Trends

Recent research has highlighted three basic demographic trends affecting the composition and movement of a typical workforce, namely:

- a continued increase in the number of women entering the workforce;
- increasing ethnic diversity, due to factors such as immigration and globalization; and
- a general aging of the working population.[1]

How should a typical organization react in the face of such trends? A growing body of literature suggests that when organizations actively manage diversity issues, there is a net benefit in terms of important organizational outcomes.[2] Organizations that seek policies of inclusion, respecting differences in background and perspectives, reap rewards in terms of increased attractiveness to a wider pool of talent, increased creativity, and improved marketing. Thus, in the minds of many researchers and business leaders, leveraging diversity is no longer a "nice to have" – it is a business imperative.

There are numerous implications of diversity for talent management and career pathing in your organization. Access to career paths, entry points, and exit points may differ according to demographic factors. Below, we explore briefly how to improve talent management for a diverse workforce.

Implications for Organizations

One important starting place for managing diversity is to understand what career barriers (real or perceived) exist for demographic subgroups of individuals. You can use both quantitative and qualitative methods (reflect back on Chapter 3) to explore the factors that mitigate advancement, movement, and entry to careers for various subgroups. Moreover, you should review your organization's talent management processes (including everything from recruiting to succession management) periodically with an eye toward potential areas of subjectivity and bias. Wherever possible, you should use objective job-related criteria in talent management systems to ensure a level playing field for all individuals.

In addition, organizational and industry leaders are often in a position to reinforce via corporate communications, policies, and reward systems that a culture of open communication, transparency, and respect for diversity is of primary importance. This is especially important in global organizations, where unanticipated cultural issues emerge. Moreover, where disadvantages for certain demographic groups occur, you should put programs in place to assist individuals via work–life balance interventions, access to training and development resources, or career planning and guidance. The box on page 132 highlights one organization that has successfully wrestled with large-scale demographic issues.

Case Scenario:
Career Planning for Older Workers at Aerospace Corporation

The Aerospace Corporation is a prime example of a company that effectively leverages an older workforce. According to its website, nearly one-half of the Aerospace Corporation's 3,500 regular, full-time workers are over 50. Among the benefits older employees receive are a phased retirement program, alternative work arrangements, such as flextime and telecommuting, and special arrangements for employees who want to continue working after they retire.

Mary M. (Marie) Waller Simmons, the company's Equal Employment Opportunity administrator, pointed out that some 90 percent of employees older than 50 developed their careers at the company.

"Most of our senior employees began their careers at Aerospace or joined the company early in their careers when they were in their 20s," she said. "Conveying the experience gained over a long career at Aerospace to newer engineers is one of the most valuable contributions made by our senior employees."

Source: Retrieved on February 20, 2008 from the Aerospace Corporation website, http://www.aero.org/news/newsitems/aarp8-21-05.html.

Trend Two – Technology

As suggested in Chapter 4, generational differences in career expectations can exist. Even if the effects of such differences are somewhat overplayed in the popular media, one thing is clear about recent generations – they have robust levels of technology literacy. For these generations, technology has become infused into every aspect of modern life. Thus, the recent "NetGen" generation (which is essentially equivalent to the Generation Y discussed in Chapter 4 and the generation following Generation Y) is immersed in a world of text messaging, social networking tools (MySpace, Facebook), and blogs.[3] How might technology change perspectives on careers? We believe there are at least three emerging phenomena, namely: new modes of networking, the rise of knowledge work, and increasingly distributed work.

First and foremost, career moves are often influenced in large part by personal networks. The rise of social networking tools, like MySpace, has thus expanded traditional career networking to the virtual domain. Individuals have started searching for job leads, exchanging career information, and even marketing themselves (some to the extent of "personal branding") via such online tools. Also of note, companies have started using online tools such as MySpace profiles to attract and recruit young talent. Companies that have used MySpace and related online tools are as diverse as the Army National Guard, Cheesecake Factory (a restaurant chain), and the Los Angeles Police Department (LAPD).

A second ongoing technological trend is the rise of knowledge work and knowledge workers. Robert Austin noted that knowledge work can be thought of as "work in which value is created primarily through manipulation of ideas or symbols, and which occurs primarily in intellectual domains."[4] Researchers such as Austin have argued that an approach that differs from traditional management approaches must be used to manage both the day-to-day work and the careers of knowledge workers. Specifically, he argues that collaboration and professionalism should be emphasized over and above incentive schemes and performance measures. He further argues for iterative work structures rather than linear, sequential ones and a mix of unstructured individual experiences and structured integration of individual work.[5] Overall, the theme in many discussions of knowledge work and workers is to emphasize the creative opportunities available for employees while de-emphasizing static, linear work structures and activities.

A third facet of technology-enabled work and careers is the increasingly available option of distributed work. As collaboration tools such as web conferencing and video conferencing improve in quality, distributed work will continue to gain momentum. For many individuals, such technologies facilitate alternative work–life arrangements, including temporary work and flexible work arrangements. Moreover, the concept of Globally Distributed Work (GDW) has emerged as an alternative to traditional off-shoring. According to recent sponsors of the Conference on the Management of Globally Distributed Work (see http://www.fiu.edu/~ciber/gdw.htm for a description), GDW is distributed geographically across nations, economies, and cultures. GDW can include globally distributed knowledge work, including offshore and near-shore research and development and information technology services, global software development, and global supply and demand chains.

Implications for Organizations

The technology trends described above suggest that you should consider ways in which 1) technology can enable more formal and information networking by employees in your organization, 2) knowledge work and workers can be managed in your organization to maximize creativity and person–job fit, and 3) flexible (and possibly distributed) work arrangements can be used by your organization to draw upon a wider array of talent.

Trend Three – Globalization and Changing Organizational Structures

Both outsourcing and globalization have fundamentally changed the way that organizations operate. Managing careers across borders can be complex for a host of reasons, not the least of which are 1) holding to key corporate strategies while adjusting to local environments and cultures, and 2) managing physical and psychological adjustment in expatriation and repatriation.[6] In addition, globalization often changes basic organizational structures and career paths. As highlighted in previous chapters, getting ahead in certain career paths may entail taking an overseas assignment, requiring adjustment for both the individual employee and his or her family. A wealth of research literature exists that highlights the factors linked to successful or unsuccessful adjustment to international assignments. These factors include how employees are selected for international assignments (selection factors), the degree of clarity in role definitions, the degree to which career implications are considered and communicated, the procedures that are used to facilitate whole family adjustment, and the adequacy of socialization processes.[7]

In addition to helping individuals and their families adjust to international environments, organizations are increasingly shifting their basic organizational structures to incorporate capabilities for globalization, adaptation to changing markets, and changes in labor supply. Changes in organizational structures mirror many of the issues raised earlier, including globalization, flatter structures, and increased networking (including strategic alliances).

Implications for Organizations

An organization's capacity to remain competitive in global and rapidly shifting markets is only as good as the adaptive capacity of its people. Thus, to help individuals manage global careers, your organization should leverage the growing body of literature on successful expatriation and repatriation and build talent management systems with such features in mind. Moreover, your organization should connect changes in organizational structures driven by globalization with career path planning and talent management. As discussed in Chapter 2, think of career paths in terms of the value proposition presented to employees and other stakeholders. The box below highlights one organization that has made great strides in managing global careers.[8]

Case Scenario:
Global Careers at HSBC

What can one of the world's largest financial groups teach us about managing global careers? Consider the HSBC group.

This institution, which operates in over eighty countries, grooms its leadership talent to work in an array of diverse cultural environments. A recent *Harvard Business Review* article called "Make Your Company a Talent Factory" highlighted some of HSBC's practices.

HSBC implements "rigorous talent processes that support strategic and cultural objectives." HSBC created a system of talent pools that track and manage the careers of high potentials. After high-potential employees have been identified, they are assigned to regional or business unit pools. Employees in these pools are given assignments within their region or line of business and, ultimately, are given positions that cross both organizational and national boundaries.

Among other interventions, HSBC established international networks among organizational leaders. So, the head of personal financial services in Hong Kong knows his or her counterpart in Mumbai, in Mexico City, in Sao Paulo, and in Vancouver. These networks facilitate the exchange of information and ideas via virtual and face-to-face meetings.

Source: Ready & Conger (2007)

Trend Four – Defining Career Success

Definitions of career success are likely to shift and morph over time, following economic, cultural, and social trends. For example, as traditional job security disappears and competition via globalization and outsourcing increases, some may define effectively managing career stress as an essential element of success.[9] In addition, with decreased organizational commitment, people may shift their inherent need for affiliation to other entities (e.g., a leader, a team, a program, or a profession).[10] Such shifting types of commitment may hold serious and long-term implications for organizational and economic dynamics that we as yet do not truly understand. For example, will individuals who optimize individual career paths that run counter to organizational commitment be viewed as self-serving? Have organizational leaders internalized the widely published message that employees are not committed?

On the flipside, one might wonder about the extent to which employees will achieve a sense of career success without organizational commitment. Changing employers and/or careers every few years may be appealing to employees in their youth, but what happens as one grows older? In addition, many individuals seek a sense of a larger purpose in their work. Thus, how organizations craft messages about social responsibility, mission, ethics, and reputation can be critical in finding and retaining talent. As stated by Harvard Business School professor Rakesh Khurana: "Ultimately the value of a company depends on how much faith people have in the organization … that faith is fostered by an ineffable and scarce element … called legitimacy."[11]

Implications for Organizations

As argued elsewhere in this book, your organization should craft a message and value proposition that foster whatever degree of commitment is available from employees. Career paths should be explicit and marketed. A sense of career purpose, aligned with the organizational mission(s), should be encouraged, and to the extent possible, you should ensure that your organization's mission and vision statements are aligned with the values of those individuals that comprise your organization's talent base. Think about and work ahead of changing definitions of career success rather than trying to catch up with implicit changes in career psychological contracts. With vigilance and a sense of strategic intent, career paths and talent management systems can be a source of sustainable competitive advantage.

The Bottom Line

Regardless of whether the trend spotting conducted in this chapter is accurate, one thing is clear: Career paths are likely to continue to become more variable, global, and oriented around individual career-seekers. Factors such as changing psychological contracts, globalization, and technology saturation simply will not go away. Thus, as argued throughout this book, you as a talent management stakeholder can be empowered in shaping career paths, structures, and systems to maximize outcomes for your organization and its employees. By attending to key leverage points and interventions, career decisions can be influenced and managed. The alternative of throwing our collective hands up in the face of presumed boundaryless careers is unacceptable. Instead, we should strive to improve the science and practice of talent management and career pathing to the point that best practices and tried and true techniques emerge. We hope that this book moves the state of practice one step closer toward this goal.

Career Path Resource List

1. **O*NET (http://online.onetcenter.org/)**
   O*NET Online is the electronic replacement for the DOT (Dictionary of Occupational Titles) that is sponsored by the U.S. Department of Labor. O*NET contains detailed information about more than eight hundred occupations that exist in the U.S. economy. O*NET provides information about a variety of occupational requirements and characteristics, such as specific knowledge, skills, abilities, and work activities associated with each occupation. O*NET can be a very useful tool for the development of career paths.

2. **CareerOneStop website (http://www.careeronestop.org/)**
   CareerOneStop is a U.S. Department of Labor-sponsored website that offers career resources and workforce information to job seekers, students, businesses, and workforce professionals to foster talent development in a global economy. The main website includes links to a number of web resources providing valuable information about careers and local work-related services. These include, for example:
   - **America's Career InfoNet.** This resource is designed to help individuals explore career opportunities to make informed employment and education choices. The website features user-friendly occupation and industry information, salary data, career videos, education resources, self-assessment tools, career exploration assistance, and other resources that support talent development in today's fast-paced global marketplace. (www.CareerInfoNet.org)

- **America's Service Locator.** This tool connects individuals to employment and training opportunities available at local One-Stop Career Centers. The website provides contact information for a range of local work-related services, including unemployment benefits, career development, and educational opportunities. (www.ServiceLocator.org)

3. **U.S. Department of Labor Competency Clearinghouse (http://www.careeronestop.org/COMPETENCYMODEL/default. aspx)**

The Competency Clearinghouse is a website designed to inform industry representatives and the public about the value of competency models, their development, and use. The site clearly articulates what competency models are and how they can be used to maintain a competitive edge in the global economy. In addition, it contains a useful tool for developing competency models, which in turn can support career path development.

4. **U.S. Bureau of Labor Statistics (http://www.bls.gov/)**

The Bureau of Labor Statistics (BLS) is the principal fact-finding agency for the Federal Government in the broad field of labor economics and labor statistics. Their website contains a wealth of information and tools relevant to career paths, including information on wages and earnings, occupational growth and outlooks, and broad economic factors that may impact career domains of interest.

The BLS website includes an electronic version of the *Occupational Outlook Handbook* (http://www.bls.gov/oco/), which contains detailed, up-to-date descriptions of occupations.

5. **Oregon Pathways Statewide Initiative (http://www.work-sourceoregon.org/index.php?option=com_content&task=category&sectionid=14&id=123&Itemid=48)**

Oregon's Pathways Statewide Initiative is designed to transform Oregon's education systems to focus on helping youth and adults attain degrees, certificates, and credentials that lead to employment in high-demand occupations, increased wage gain, and lifelong learning. The Oregon initiative is a good example of cooperation among stakeholders on initiatives that guide career seekers along career paths.

The website for the initiative contains links to over a hundred community college-oriented career pathways. Your organization or industry may find information in these pathways helpful when developing career paths.

Notes

Chapter 1

1 Walker (1992)
2 Feldman (2002)

Chapter 2

1 Cardy, Miller & Ellis (2007)
2 Feldman & Ng (2007)
3 McDonald & Hite (2005)
4 Baruch (2006)
5 Baruch (2006)
6 Hedge, Borman & Bourne (2006)

Chapter 3

1 Nalbantian, Guzzo, Kieffer & Doherty (2004)
2 Baker, Gibbs & Holmstrom (1994)
3 Nalbantian, Guzzo, Kieffer & Doherty (2004)
4 Equal Employment Opportunity Commission (1978)
5 Buster, Roth & Bobko (2005)
6 Levine, Maye, Ulm & Gordon (1997)
7 U.S. Department of Labor, Bureau of Labor Statistics (2005)
8 Brannick & Levine (2002)
9 National Center for O*NET Development (n.d.)

Chapter 4

1 Sullivan, Carden & Martin (1998)
2 Raimy (2002)
3 Badal (2006)
4 Armour (2005)
5 Tamminen & Moilanen (2004)
6 NAS Recruitment Communications (2006)
7 Levering & Moskowitz (2008)
8 Kristof-Brown, Zimmerman & Johnson (2005)
9 Levering & Moskowitz (2008)

Chapter 5

1 Levering & Moskowitz (2008)
2 Greer (1995)
3 Rothwell, Jackson, Knight & Lindholm (2005)
4 Nalbantian, Guzzo, Kieffer & Doherty (2004)
5 Nalbantian, Guzzo, Kieffer & Doherty (2004)
6 Byham, Smith & Paese (2000)

Chapter 6

1 Public Works and Economic Development Act of 1965
2 Jenkins (2006)
3 Jenkins (2006)
4 Jenkins & Spence (2006)
5 Jenkins (2006)
6 Agrawal et al. (2007)
7 About Oregon Statewide Pathways Initiative
8 Greenberg & Cultice (1997)
9 North Carolina O*NET Center (1998)

Chapter 7

1 Baruch (2006)
2 Baruch (2006)
3 Burke & Ng (2006)
4 Austin (2002)
5 Austin (2002)
6 Baruch (2006)

7 Fisher, Wasserman & Palthe (2007)
8 Ready & Conger (2007)
9 Baruch (2006)
10 Baruch (2006)
11 Reier (2005)

References

About Oregon Statewide Pathways Initiative. Retrieved October 10, 2007 from http://www.worksourceoregon.org.

Agrawal, A., Alssid, J. L., Bird, K., Goldberg, M., Hess, S., Jacobs, J., Jenkins, D., Joseph, G., Kazis, R., King-Simms, S., Laprade, N., Long, S., Maduro, M., Petty, J., McClenney, K., McKeehan, P., McKenney, J., Mendoza, I., Meyer, A., Pfeiffer, M., Poppe, N., Rubin, J., Snyder, D., Taylor, J., & Warford, L. (2007). *Career pathways as a systematic framework: Rethinking education for student success in college and careers.* Phoenix, AZ: League for Innovation in the Community College.

Armour, S. (2005, November 8). Generation Y: They've arrived at work with a new attitude. *USA Today,* Money section.

Austin, R. (2002, April). Managing knowledge workers: Evolving practices and trends. *Science: Next Wave.* Retrieved from: http://sciencecareers. sciencemag.org/career_development/previous_issues/articles/1470/ managing_knowledge_workers.

Badal, J. (2006, July 24). 'Career Path' programs help retain workers. *The Wall Street Journal Online.*

Baker, G., Gibbs, M., & Holmstrom, B. (1994). The internal economics of the firm: Evidence from personnel data. *The Quarterly Journal of Economics, 109,* 881–919.

Baruch, Y. (2006). Career development in organizations and beyond: Balancing traditional and contemporary viewpoints. *Human Resource Management Review, 16*(2), 125–138.

Brannick, M. T., & Levine, E. L. (2002) *Job analysis: Methods, research and applications for human resource management in the new millennium.* Thousand Oaks, CA: Sage.

Burke, R. J., & Ng, E. S. W. (2006). The changing nature of work and organizations: Implications for human resource management. *Human Resource
Management Review, 16*(2), 86–94.

Buster, M. A., Roth, P. L., & Bobko, P. (2005). A process for content validation of education and experienced-based minimum qualifications: An
approach resulting in Federal court approval. *Personnel Psychology, 58,*
771–799.

Byham, W. C., Smith, A. B., & Paese, M. J. (2000). *Grow your own leaders.*
Bridgeville, PA: DDI Press.

Cardy, R. L., Miller, J. S., & Ellis, A. D. (2007). Employee equity as an HRM
framework. *Human Resource Management Review, 17,* 140–151.

Equal Employment Opportunity Commission. (1978). Uniform Guidelines
on Employee Selection Procedures. *Federal Register, 43,* 38290–
38315.

Feldman, D. C. (2002). Stability in the midst of change: A developmental
perspective on the study of careers. In D. C. Feldman (Ed.), *Work careers:
A developmental perspective* (pp. 3–26). San Francisco: Jossey-Bass.

Feldman, D. C., & Ng, T. W. H. (2007). Careers: Mobility, embeddedness,
and success. *Journal of Management, 33,* 350–377.

Fisher, S. L., Wasserman, M. E., & Palthe, J. (2007). Management practices
for on-site consultants: Lessons learned from the expatriate experience.
Consulting Psychology Journal, 59(1), 17–29.

Greenberg, L., & Cultice, J. M. (1997). Forecasting the need for physicians
in the United States: The Health Resources and Services Administration's
physician requirements model. *Health Services Research, 31*(6), 723–
737.

Greer, C. R. (1995). *Strategy and human resources: A general managerial
perspective.* Englewood Cliffs, NJ: Prentice Hall.

Hedge, J. W., Borman, W. C., & Bourne, M. J. (2006). Designing a system
for career development and advancement in the U.S. Navy. *Human
Resource Management Review, 16,* 340–355.

Jenkins, D. (2006). *Career pathways: Aligning public resources to support
individual and regional economic advancement in the knowledge economy.*
New York: Workforce Strategy Center.

Jenkins, D., & Spence, C. (2006). *The career pathways how-to guide.* New
York: Workforce Strategy Center.

Kristof-Brown, A. L., Zimmerman, R. D., & Johnson, E. C. (2005). Conse-
quences of individuals' fit at work: A meta-analysis of person–job,
person–organization, person–group and person–supervisor fit. *Personnel
Psychology, 58*(2), 281–342.

Levering, R., & Moskowitz, M. (2008, February 4). The 100 best companies
to work for 2008. *Fortune, 157*(2), 75–94.

Levine, E. L., Maye, D. M., Ulm, R. A., & Gordon, T. R. (1997). A methodology of developing and validating minimum qualifications (MQs). *Personnel Psychology, 50,* 1009–1023.

McDonald, K. S., & Hite, L. M. (2005). Reviving the relevance of career development in human resource development. *Human Resource Development Review, 4*(4), 418–439.

Nalbantian, H. R., Guzzo, R. A., Kieffer, D., & Doherty, J. (2004). *Play to your strengths: Managing your internal labor markets for lasting competitive advantage.* New York: McGraw-Hill.

NAS Recruitment Communications. (2006). *Generation Y: The Millennials. Ready or not, here they come.* Cleveland, OH: Author.

National Center for O*NET Development (n.d.). *O*NET Online help.* Retrieved July 15, 2007 from http://online.onetcenter.org/help/onet/.

North Carolina O*NET Center. (1998). *Summary report: O*NET nearest neighbor matrix and related occupations projects.* Raleigh, NC: Author.

Public Works and Economic Development Act of 1965, *42 U.S.C. § 3121.*

Raimy, E. (2002, January). Ladders of success. *Human Resource Executive, 16*(1), 36–41.

Ready, D. A., & Conger, J. A. (2007). Make your company a talent factory. *Harvard Business Review, 85*(6), 68–77.

Reier, S. (2005, March 12). Investing: Moral values do matter. *International Herald Tribune.* Retrieved from: http://www.iht.com/articles/2005/03/11/yourmoney/minvest12.php.

Rothwell, W. J., Jackson, R. D., Knight, S. C., & Lindholm, J. E. (2005). *Career planning and succession management: Developing your organization's talent – for today and tomorrow.* Westport, CT: Praeger.

Sullivan, S. E., Carden, W. A., & Martin, D. F. (1998). Careers in the next millennium: Directions for future research. *Human Resource Management Review, 8*(2), 165–185.

Tamminen, H., & Moilanen, R. (2004). *The significance of HRD for young and older employees: A psychological contract perspective.* Paper presented at the Society for Human Resource Management Conference.

U.S. Department of Labor, Bureau of Labor Statistics (2005). *Occupational Outlook Handbook, 2006–2007.* Washington, DC: Author.

Walker, J. W. (1992). Career paths in flexible organizations. In D. H. Montross & C. J. Shinkman (Eds.), *Career development: Theory and practice* (pp. 387–400). Springfield, IL: Charles C. Thomas.

Name Index

Note: Page numbers followed by n and a number indicate endnotes

Agrawal, A.   120, 144n6
Armour, S.   144n4
Austin, R.   133, 144n4, 144n5

Badal, J.   71, 144n3
Baker, G.   35, 143n2
Baruch, Y.   31, 143n4, 143n5,
    144n1, 144n2, 144n6, 145n9,
    145n10
Bobko, P.   143n5
Borman, W. C.   32, 143n6
Bourne, M. J.   32, 143n6
Brannick, M. T.   143n8
Burke, R. J.   144n3
Buster, M. A.   143n5
Byham, W. C.   144n6

Carden, W. A.   70, 144n1
Cardy, R. L.   143n1
Conger, J. A.   135, 145n8
Cultice, J. M.   144n8

Doherty, J.   143n1, 143n3, 144n4,
    144n5

Ellis, A. D.   143n1

Feldman, D. C.   143n2,
    143n2
Fisher, S. L.   145n7

Gaius Petronius   32
Gibbs, M.   35, 143n2
Gordon, T. R.   143n6
Greenberg, L.   144n8
Greer, C. R.   144n2
Guzzo, R. A.   143n1, 143n3,
    144n4, 144n5

Hedge, J. W.   32, 143n6
Hite, L. M.   143n3
Holmstrom, B.   35, 143n2

Jackson, R. D.   144n3
Jenkins, D.   118, 119, 144n2,
    144n3, 144n4, 144n5
Johnson, E. C.   144n8

Khurana, R.   136
Kieffer, D.   143n1, 143n3, 144n4,
    144n5
Knight, S. C.   144n3
Kristof-Brown, A. L.   144n8

Levine, E. L.   143n6, 143n8
Levering, R.   144n7, 144n9, 144n1
Lindholm, J. E.   144n3

Martin, D. F.   70, 144n1
Maye, D. M.   143n6
McDonald, K. S.   143n3
Miller, J. S.   143n1
Moilanen, R.   144n5
Moskowitz, M.   144n7, 144n9,
    144n1

Nalbantian, H. R.   35, 37, 93, 94,
    143n1, 143n3, 144n4, 144n5
Ng, E. S. W.   144n3
Ng, T. W. H.   143n2

Paese, M. J.   144n6
Palthe, J.   145n7

Raimy, E.   144n2
Ready, D. A.   145n8
Reier, S.   145n11
Roth, P. L.   143n5
Rothwell, W. J.   144n3

Smith, A. B.   144n6
Spence, C.   119, 144n4
Sullivan, S. E.   70, 144n1

Tamminen, H.   144n5

Ulm, R. A.   143n6

Walker, J. W.   143n1
Wasserman, M. E.   145n7

Zimmerman, R. D.
    144n8

Subject Index

Aerospace Corporation 132
aging work population 72–3, 130, 132
alignment
different interests 41, 61, 62, 64
education systems and labor market 119–20
America's Career Infonet 44, 139
America's Service Locator 140
Army National Guard 133
assessment
personal attributes 64–5
professional and legal guidelines 53–4
promotion evaluation 101–2
simulation-based 103

Baby Boomers, retiring 93
blogs 132
boundaryless careers 31, 137
breadth of knowledge 16, 63
Burger King 72

CareerOneStop website 54, 139
see also Competency Clearinghouse

career path guides, sample 5–16
career path outcomes 29–30
career path patterns 27–9
career path tools, purpose driven 40
career paths
attributes 26–9
centerpiece of effective talent management systems 19, 20 (fig), 29, 42, 66
conceptual model of 23–32
cross-occupation 126–7
definition 2–5
development methods 42
economic development and organizational compared 124–5
economic development perspective 118–25
education and 119–24
five fundamental components 4–5, 47–63
focus and content 40–4
future-focused 37–8
how to construct 39–67
implementation 65–7

career paths (*cont'd*)
  importance of   4
  industry perspective   108–18
  information sources   40–1
  no guarantee for promotion
    66–7
  non-linear   70
  not only path to success   66
  organizational perspective   24,
    101
  purpose-driven   40–4, 116–17
  strategic workforce planning
    92–5
  training and development
    purposes   83
career pathways framework   119–
  20, 124
career roadmap/atlas   86
career success, definition   136–7
career success factors
  constructing a career path
    60–3
  discussion about   50
  industry perspective   118
  questions   26–7, 61
  sample career path guide   15
career value propositions   24–5
certifications, occupation specific
  54   *see also* qualifications
changing organizational structures
  134–5
Cheesecake Factory   133
communication
  clear and open with employees
    70
  culture of open   131
  project plan   46–7
  regarding high-potential
    program   98–9
community colleges   119, 120
  career pathways   121 (fig), 122–
    3 (fig)

competencies
  constructing a career path
    56–60
  definition   56
  detail of information varies   57
  gathering information   37, 51
  industry perspective   109
  and movement   64
  relevant to retention   81
  sample career path guide   6–10,
    11, 12, 13–15, 16
  training and development
    83, 86
  transferability and marketability
    70
  use of surveys   57–8
Competency Clearinghouse   58,
  59, 140
competency gaps   25
contract, implied or psychological
  31, 69–70, 137
critical developmental experiences
  constructing a career path
    54–6
  examples   55
  fundamental component   4, 47
  gathering information   37–8
  industry perspective   117–18
  questions to ask   56
  sample career path guide   6, 7,
    10–11, 12, 13, 14–15
cross-geography experience   11,
  16, 63
cross-occupation requirements
  126–7
current job, importance of   66

demographic trends   130–1
derailers   65
Dictionary of Occupational Titles
  (DOT)   *see* O*NET
diversity, advantages of   130–1

EchoStar   71, 72
Economic Development
    Administration   108
economic development initiatives
    108–9, 118–25
education and training
    alignment with labor market
        119–20
    central focus of economic
        development paths   125
employee development, SEC case
    scenario   43
employees
    commitment/loyalty   74, 80,
        129, 136
    competition for highly skilled   109
    connecting to organization   69–
        72, 91–2
    using career paths to improve
        promotion decisions   81–2,
        84–5
    using career paths to retain
        80–1
enablers   65
entrepreneurs, career path pattern
    28–9
ethnic diversity   130–1

Facebook   132
Federal Government contractors,
    point of contact   39, 46
Five Vector Model (5VM)   32
flexible work arrangements   133
focus groups
    gathering information from   37,
        38–9, 51
    representatives of industry   117
folk theories, what leads to success
    34, 41, 61
    using HR data to test   62
Fortune, 100 Best Companies to
    Work For   74, 79, 92

generalist, career path pattern   28
Generation Y   72–3, 132
geographic regions   107, 118, 127
Geo-Skills Profile   127
global economy   107, 118, 119,
    126, 128
globalization   130, 134–5, 136,
    137
Globally Distributed Work (GDW)
    133–4
Google   92

high-potential leadership talent
    95–9
    communications regarding
        98–9
    criteria for identifying   96–7
    HSBC   135
    myths regarding   96
holistic management of careers
    23–4
Home Builders Institute (HBI)
    Careers Campaign   44, 110–15,
        116 (fig)
hourly jobs   71–2
HSBC, managing global careers
    135
human capital strategy   37–8
human resources (HR) databases
    34, 35, 41
    analyzing   49–50, 62
    electronic form   49
human resource (HR) systems,
    component of talent
    management   23–4

industry associations   108–9
integrated career management, US
    Navy   32
Internal Labor Market (ILM)
    analyses   35–7, 93
international assignments   134

interviews
  career success factors
    information from 62–3
  competency information
    gathered from 59–60
  criteria for selecting participants
    38, 41–2, 51
  formal 51
  gathering information from 34,
    37, 38–9, 48
  initial 50
  job experts 56
  representatives of industry
    117

job analysis, competency
  information gathered from
  58–9

knowledge and skills, marketable
  118, 126
knowledge work/ers 74, 107, 118,
  119, 127, 132, 133, 134

Labor Market Analyses 35, 125–6
League for Innovation in the
  Community College 120
legal department, consulting with
  high-potential programs 97
  hiring 77
  promotion 82
logistic regression analyses 35–7
Los Angeles Police Department
  (LAPD) 133
loyalty and commitment, employee
  74, 80, 129, 136

managers
  formal interviews with 51
  performance/development
    planning 78–9, 87–9
  promotion decisions 81–5

strategic plan of organization
  37–8, 51–2
  use of career paths by 70–1
movement of individuals over time
  5, 25, 28–9, 35–6, 41
  explicit focus on 64
  using HR databases 35–7, 49, 62
MySpace 132, 133

National Association of Home
  Builders 44, 110
National Retail Federation 47
  Career Profiles 110, 111–15 (fig)

Occupational Outlook Handbook
  44, 54
  electronic version of 140
off-shoring 3 *see also* Globally
  Distributed Work (GDW)
onboarding 77–8
O*NET system 48, 58, 63, 139
  competency information
    gathered from 59
  cross-occupation requirements
    126–7
  industry-wide information 117
  optimal length of time in a position
    16, 63
Oregon Pathways Statewide
  Initiative 120, 140–1
organizational change 41
  response to globalization 134–5
  SEC case scenario 43
outcomes 29–30
  maximizing in career path
    construction 40–1
outsourcing 3, 134, 136

personal attributes 64–5
  myth regarding 96
personnel decisions, guidelines on
  53–4

Play to Your Strengths   94
point of contact (POC), career path
    project   39, 46, 50, 51, 60, 63
professional associations   108, 110
Project Management Institute   46
project plan   46
promotion   81–5
    evaluating readiness for   101–2
    folk theories   41, 62
    Internal Labor Market Analysis
        (ILM)   35–7
    keeping those not yet ready
        102–5
    minimum qualifications   53
    non selection for   83
    organizational decision makers
        62

qualifications
    constructing a career path   53–4
    fundamental component   4
    gathering information   37
    identification and validation   54
    industry perspective   109–10,
        117
    relevant to retention   81
    requirements not recommended
        for career path project   54, 77
    sample career path guide   7, 10,
        12, 13, 14
    selection and promotion
        decisions   53–4
Quicken Loans   78–9 (fig), 79–80,
    92

recruitment   73–80
regional economic development
    108, 119, 120
retention   80–1
    EchoStar   71–2
    entry-level positions   74
    high-potential staff   95

see also loyalty and commitment,
    employee
role play   65   *see also* simulation-
    based assessment

salary information   63
    industry career paths   118
sample career path guide   6–16
Securities and Exchange
    Commission (SEC), case
    scenario   43
selection procedures, guidelines on
    53–4
self-insight   64–5
sequential list of roles   4, 7, 10, 48
    (fig)
    most fundamental component of
        career path   47
    questions to ask   52
    relevant to retention   80
simulation-based assessment   103
skills, transferable versus
    organization-specific   70, 129
skills gap *see* competency gaps
social networking   132, 133
sources of information   34–9
    career path purpose determine   40
    competences   57–60
    economic development purposes
        124–5
    HR data   49–50
    industry associations   110
    industry career paths   117–18
    salaries   63
    US Census Bureau   127
specialist, career path pattern   28
stakeholders
    career path project   39–40
    communication with   46–7
    explaining benefits of career
        paths   66
    identifying   39

strategic plan of organization 37,
51–2, 91–2
initial interviews about 50
strategic workforce planning 92–5
alignment of interests 41
subjectivity and bias 131
success factors
decision-maker opinions 62
explored in interviews and
workshops 62–3
fundamental component 4
industry perspective 118
path attributes and questions
26–7, 60–1
retaining employees 81
sample career path guide 15
succession management 42, 99–105
evaluating readiness 102, 103
highest expectations placed upon
high potentials 101
keeping those not yet ready 102–5
surveys
competences and qualification
information source 37, 57–8
representatives from industry
117

talent management systems
career paths centerpiece of 19,
20 (fig), 29, 42
diversity and 131
integrating career paths into
69–105
talent management, trends
impacting
changing definitions of career
success 136–7
demographic 130–2
globalization and changing
organizational structures
134–5
technology 132–4

target jobs
gather information about 48–9
identify 44–6
initial interviews about 50
interview/workshop participants
38
qualifications for 54
technology 132–4
text messaging 132
training and development
Business/Role/Self model 86
(fig), 87, 98
career paths designed primarily
for 83, 86
individual development plans 87
ineffective systems 25
linking competences to 42, 57, 83

*Uniform Guidelines on Employee
Selection Procedures* 54
union representatives, as
stakeholders 40, 47
US Census Bureau, source of
information 127
US Department of Labor
American Career InfoNet 44,
139
Bureau of Labor Statistics website
63, 117, 118, 127, 140
CareerOneStop website 54, 139
Competency Clearinghouse 58,
59, 140
O*NET system 48, 58, 59, 63,
126, 139
US Navy 32

wages *see* salary information
"war for talent" 23
web-based career path resources
110
web-based development resource
83

Whole Foods Market   74–7, 92
  career website   75–6 (fig)
women, number entering
  workforce   130
workforce planning *see* strategic
  workforce planning
work–life balance   129, 131, 133
workshops   50–1
  competency information
    gathered from   59–60
  criteria for selecting participants
    38, 51

information gathering   37, 38–
  9, 48, 51
qualifications questions
  54
success factors information from
  62–3

younger workers   73
  more mobile than ever   93
  tagged as high potentials
    96
  technology literacy   132